VOICES IN LITERAT

GOLD

Student Journal
with
Activity Masters

Standards-based Edition

Mary Lou McCloskey
Lydia Stack

HEINLE & HEINLE

THOMSON LEARNING ™

United States   Australia   Canada   Mexico   Singapore   Spain   United Kingdom

Vice President, Editorial Director ESL/ELT: Nancy Leonhardt
Director of School Publishing: Edward Lamprich

Development Editors: Nancy Jordan, Amy Lawler, Donna Schaffer, and Janet Raskin
Editorial Assistant: Sarah Barnicle
Director of Global ESL Training and Development: Evelyn Nelson
Marketing Manager: John Ade
Production Editor: Michael Burggren

Manufactured in the United States of America.

ISBN: 0-8384-2296-9

1 2 3 4 5 6 7 8 9 10   04 03 02 01

Contents

Unit 1: Style

Unit 2: Suspense

Unit 3: Love

Unit 4: Advice

Introduction

Welcome to the *Student Journal with Activity Masters for Voices in Literature Gold*. In this component, you will find Activity Masters, as well as an End-of-Selection project, for every literature selection in the Student Text.

Activity Masters

The Activity Masters develop the skills outlined in the standards—reading, writing, listening, speaking, and viewing. At the bottom of each Activity Master, teachers will find additional strategies to highlight and integrate the standards. You will find icons indicating the Making Connections CD-ROM and The Newbury House Dictionary CD-ROM when dictionary use and vocabulary acquisition practice will help the students.

 The AM icon appears in the Student Text and Teacher's Guide as an indication of when it is appropriate to use an Activity Master from the Student Journal.

End-of-Unit Writing

Each unit has an End-of-Unit Writing activity that provides a writing prompt and clear directions for student writing. These activities also provide testing practice. Teachers may duplicate these pages as transparencies for whole-class and group work.

End-of-Selection Projects

After each literature selection there is an End-of-Selection Project which integrates skills outlined in the standards. These projects:

- develop the selection and task-related vocabulary

- engage students in projects that tie the literature and skills together

- provide tips and checklists for students to check their progress

- provide opportunities for using interactive multimedia technology with the *Making Connections CD-ROM* and *The Newbury House Dictionary CD-ROM*

 These CD-ROMs are designed to complement students' learning. Look for these icons for suggestions of when to use them.

The Best Ways to Use the Student Journal with Activity Masters

- Work the pages in class treating the Student Journal as an extension of the Student Text.

- Introduce the pages in class and assign them as pairwork or individual homework.

- Have students work on their own, especially during self-evaluation, using the checklists.

We wish you and your students a successful and exciting learning experience.

ACTIVITY MASTER 1

Use with student text page 4.

Family Interview

Ask an older family member these questions. Use another language if you like. Write down the answers and/or draw pictures of the answers.

1. What clothing did you wear when you were my age?
2. Where did you live then?
3. What did your parents do to make a living?
4. What clothing did your parents wear when they were my age?
5. Where did your parents live then?
6. How did their parents make a living?

Listening/Speaking. Students discuss ways that their lives are different from those of the people they interviewed.
Writing/inquiry/research. Students write to clarify their ideas in the interview. Students can then represent their information visually through pictures.

MY MOCCASINS HAVE NOT WALKED

Use with student text page 8.

Styles of Generations

1. Summarize the information from Activity Master 1 on page 1.

2. Use the chart below to compare yourself, your parents, and your grandparents. Use key words, not sentences, and include many specific details and words.

	What clothing did they wear?	Where did they live?	How did they make a living?
My family			
My parents' families when my parents were young			
My grandparents' families when my grandparents were young			

Write drawing on cultural background.   Ask students to use their background to provide connections to the poem.

Use with student text page 9.

Repetition

1. Poets often make sure their words stay in the reader's memory by using repetition. For example:

   My moccasins have not walked
   My leggings have not brushed

2. Find other examples of repetition in the text. List them below:

   _____

   _____

   _____

   _____

   _____

   _____

   _____

3. Write a poem about your own ancestors using the pattern: *My _____ have/has not _____.*

   _____

   _____

   _____

   _____

   _____

   _____

   _____

   _____

   _____

   _____

Listening/Speaking. Ask students to read their poems aloud. Have others listen for devices such as repetition and then tell how the devices helped them better understand the poem.

Write a personal response to literature. Have students write using the style of repetition to match the poem.

Use with student text pages 5–7.

Clothing Then and Now: A Report of Information

Words to Know

ancestors   wool   fur   leather   Colonial

Project Goal: Duke Redbird, a Native American, wrote "My moccasins have not walked." He wrote it about his **ancestors** and included details about the clothing they wore. This project will take you back to **Colonial** America. At that time, many people wore clothing made from **fur** and **leather**. You will find out about clothing in Colonial times, write a report, and present your information to your class.

1. Work in a small group. What did people wear in Colonial America? Why did they wear those kinds of clothes? Look in books or encyclopedias, or watch videos about Colonial times. Use indexes to find key words. Skim to find information about the clothes. Look at pictures.
   Reading tip: Make a list of words that are new to you and use a dictionary to write a definition. Ask for help if you are not sure how to say the words.

2. Write a report summarizing your information. Choose three pieces of clothing. Write a description and draw a picture of each. Who wore the clothing and why? Did they wear it every day or just on special days? What was it made out of? What does the clothing tell you about the culture and the time?
   Writing tip: Make a chart like the one on page 2. Take notes, listing only the most important words. Use adjectives. For your final draft, use complete sentences.

3. Prepare a short oral presentation about one piece of clothing from your report. Compare and contrast clothing people wear today with clothing from Colonial America. Invite others to ask questions.
   Listening/Speaking tip: Practice your report out loud with your group. Ask yourself whether you speak clearly or too slowly. Check your pronunciation.

Extend: The next time you read a selection about a different period in history, follow similar steps to find out more about the time. This will help you better understand what you read.

Check your progress:

Listening/Speaking: Did you pronounce new words correctly? Did knowing words about Colonial America help you understand the reports? Did you ask and answer questions?

Reading: Did you take notes on the information you found about Colonial America? Did you skim and scan for ideas in the books you used and summarize the information?

Writing: Did you write in complete sentences? Did you use adjectives to describe the clothing? Did you put the adjectives before the name of the clothing? (*a **leather** jacket, a **wool** coat*)

Viewing: Did you find pictures of clothing from the past? Did you find pictures of clothing now? Did you explain how they are the same or different?

Learn more about clothing with The Newbury House Dictionary CD-ROM, Unit 22. Develop vocabulary and language about clothing with the Making Connections CD-ROM, Unit 4.

UNIT 1: STYLE

Quickwrite

1. Think about a time when you were embarrassed. What happened? How did you feel?

2. Write for five to ten minutes, writing everything that comes into your head about this embarrassing experience. Write down as many ideas as you can, without worrying about your spelling, grammar, and punctuation. You can correct your work later.

_____

_____

_____

_____

_____

_____

_____

_____

_____

_____

_____

_____

_____

3. When you finish writing, share your draft with a group of three or four classmates. Talk about the situations you have heard.

4. Select your group's favorite story and share it with the entire class.

Writing a personal, autobiographical narrative. Ask students to write about an embarrassing situation using **Quickwrite** as a pre-writing strategy.

Food Similes

1. Look at the picture of broccoli below. Does the picture remind you of something? Write a phrase and draw a picture about the phrase in the box below the broccoli.

Food:	Broccoli	Potatoes	Parsley	Mushrooms	Grapes
Reminds me of:					

2. Write a simile about each phrase. Don't forget to use *like* or *as* in your simile.

Broccoli is like falling trees.

_____

_____

_____

_____

_____

_____

Listening/Speaking. Have students work in pairs. Have them take turns reading their similes aloud and giving feedback.
Writing personal forms (similes) in response to literature. After reading "Eleven" by Sandra Cisneros, have students practice writing similes using "like" and "as" from the picture prompts above.

ACTIVITY
6
MASTER

Use with student text page 17.

UNIT 1: STYLE

Onion Chart

In each part of the onion, write something that happened to you at that age.

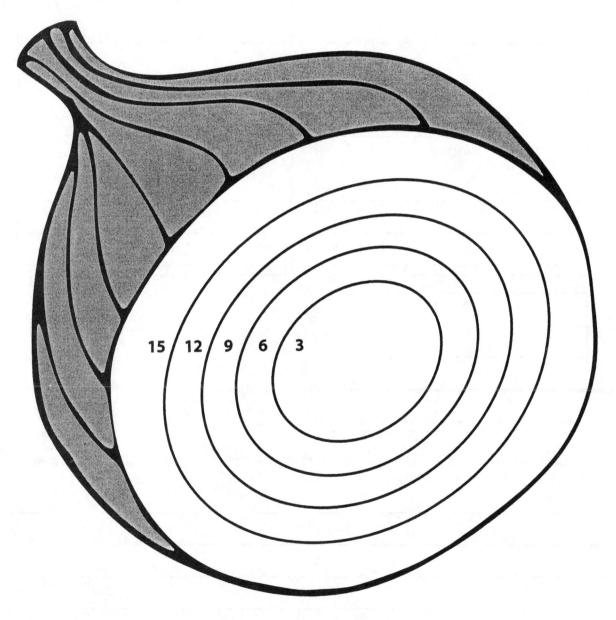

15 12 9 6 3

Writing/autobiographical narrative.   Students use Sandra Cisneros' model in "Eleven" to write, organizing their own ideas in a logical progression using the **pre-writing strategy** of a graphic organizer (Onion Chart) above.

Use with student text page 17.

ACTIVITY **7** MASTER

A Childhood Memoir

1. Look at the "onion ring" on Activity Master 6 on page 7.

2. For each age, write a few phrases that describe what you might have thought about or acted like at that age.

Age 3	Age 6

Age 9	Age 12

Age 15

3. Choose one of the ages. Write about an event in your past from your point of view at that age. Use another piece of paper when you run out of room here.

_____

_____

_____

_____

_____

Enhancing the reading experience. Students listen to the selection on the cassette, then practice reading aloud. They listen for pauses and exaggerated intonation for key words and practice this when reading aloud.
Writing/purpose and process: autobiographical narrative. Students use the graphic organizer above to organize their own ideas in a progressive order. Refer to Sandra Cisneros' selection, "Eleven."

Use with student text pages 11–15.

What It Means to be a Teenager: A Guidebook to Being One!

Words to Know

similes	teens	experiences	problems
interests	feelings	pressures	hang out

Project Goal: You just read a story about how it feels to be eleven. The writer used the word "like" to compare her **feelings**. How does it feel to be a teenager? You will make a guidebook to being a teenager. You can share it with others who are not yet teenagers.

Work in groups of three or four.

1. Think and talk about what it means to be a teenager. If it helps, use **similes** with the word "like" to make your meaning clear. What do "typical **teens**" do? Where do they go to school? For how long? What do they study? What do they wear, eat, and talk about? Where do they **hang out**? Watch favorite TV shows about teenagers. What **problems** and **pressures** do they have? What feelings do they have? Look through magazines for pictures of teenagers.
   Speaking tip: Be sure to speak up in the discussion. Use examples from TV shows, magazines, ads, and your own experiences, too.

2. Make word webs about the feelings, problems, and **interests** of teenagers. Choose one aspect of being a teenager that interests you. For example, write a paragraph about feelings. Use details from your webs to support your main ideas. Be sure to include your own **experiences.** Use similes with the word "like." Read your paragraph aloud to your group. After each person reads, tell what you liked about what you heard.
   Writing tip: Use editing checklists and peer editing to review your writing.

3. Do some research about facts about teenagers. How many teenagers are there in this country? What kind of music do they listen to? How many go to college? Write about your findings.
   Reading tip: Use almanacs and other resources at your library to find facts about teenagers today. Choose categories you want to find out about. Look up key words.

4. Gather what each group wrote and any pictures in *A Guidebook to Being a Teenager*.

Extend: Create other guidebooks, such as *A Guidebook to Being a Soccer Player*.

Check your progress:

Listening/Speaking: Did you listen to what others said so that you could add to the discussion about teenagers?

Reading: Did you choose categories and look up key words when you did your research?

Writing: Did you organize and use main ideas and details from your word webs?

Viewing: Did you watch TV shows and look at magazines and ads about teenagers?

Learn language about emotions with The Newbury House Dictionary CD-ROM, Unit 21. Learn to express opinions with the Making Connections CD-ROM, Unit 2.

Use with student text page 18.

UNIT 1: STYLE

Masks

For many different reasons, people sometimes choose to hide their feelings. In "Eleven," Rachel was upset because she couldn't hide her feelings, but instead cried in front of everyone. Have you ever been in a situation where you felt like crying but instead smiled, or where you felt angry but instead put on a calm face?

1. Think about that situation.
2. Discuss your experience with a small group of classmates.
3. Draw two masks to show the way you felt and the face you showed.
4. You may choose to share your masks with the class and/or put them in a class display.

MY MASKS
A brief description of the situation:

The way I felt	The face I showed (or wished I'd shown)

Writing and ESOL pre-writing strategy. Have students draw two pictures: one showing how they felt in a situation and the other showing the "mask" face they showed to others.

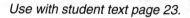

Use with student text page 23.

ACTIVITY 9 MASTER

Finding the Rhyme

1. Find the rhyming words in the poem "We Wear the Mask"—for example, *lies* and *eyes*.

2. Draw a line under each rhyming word you find.

We wear the mask that grins and lies,
It hides our cheeks and shades our eyes—
This debt we pay to human guile;
With torn and bleeding hearts we smile,
And mouth with myriad subtleties.

Why should the world be overwise,
In counting all our tears and sighs?
Nay, let them only see us, while
    We wear the mask.

We smile, but, O great Christ, our cries
To thee from tortured souls arise.
We sing, but oh the clay is vile
Beneath our feet, and long the mile;
But let the world dream otherwise,
    We wear the mask!

---

3. Label each set of rhyming words with a letter, starting with "a," then "b," then "c." For example, the words *lies* and *eyes* should both have an "a" above them. Put a "b" above the next set of rhyming words in the stanza. Begin again with the letter "a" when you start a new stanza.

4. What is the pattern of this poem?

   STANZA 1:_____

   STANZA 2:_____

   STANZA 3:_____

5. What is the effect of these rhyming words?

   _____
   _____
   _____
   _____

Listening/Speaking and Reading elements of the text. Have students work in pairs to analyze the effects of the **rhyming words**.

Enhancing the reading experience. Have students listen to the selection on the cassette, then practice reading aloud. Students should listen for pauses and exaggerated intonation of key words and practice this when they read aloud.

WE WEAR THE MASK

Use with student text page 23.

Rhyming Couplets

1. Review what you wrote or drew about masks on Activity Master 8 on page 10. Close your eyes, and search for an image or picture in your mind that you would like to write about.

2. Think of as many rhyming words as you can to describe the picture in your mind.

3. Draft your rhyming couplets. A *rhyming couplet* is two lines that rhyme at the end of each line.

_____

_____

_____

_____

_____

_____

_____

_____

_____

_____

_____

_____

_____

4. Share your couplets with a group of classmates, and give one another feedback. Use Activity Master 96 (Responding to Peers' Writing: EQS) to help you.

5. Revise your couplets and write them on another piece of paper. Draw or find pictures in magazines that illustrate the couplets you wrote. Publish illustrated couplets in a class book or post them on the wall as a class display.

Listening/Speaking and Reading elements of the text. When students share their couplets, be sure they read them aloud and ask the students to selectively listen for the couplets.
Sound/symbol relationships. Have students find words with the same vowel sounds. Point out the variation in letter patterns that represent a sound. For example, point out that the spellings *-ie*, *eye*, *-igh* and *-ile* stand for the vowel sound heard in the word *tight*.

Use with student text pages 19–21.

Mask Museum Tour: An Art Project

Words to Know

mask	scary	ritual	theater	quality
disguise	represent	dance	culture	tour guide

Project Goal: The poem you just read is about the **"masks"** people wear every day—the expressions that hide their feelings. Sometimes, people wear real masks, too. You will research, create, and write about a mask. You'll create a Mask Museum! Will you be a **tour guide** or a visitor? You'll discover why people have worn masks through the years. Work in small groups. Take turns being visitors to the museum and tour guides.

1. First, list reasons people wear masks today—for example, to **disguise** themselves, to look **scary**. Then look in books or encyclopedias for groups that have worn masks through the years. Ancient Greek actors wore masks in plays. In some African **cultures**, dancers wear masks when they perform **ritual dances**. Find out what masks **represent** and why they are important. Do they represent animals, people, or gods?

    Reading tip: Look up key words like *mask, Greece, theater,* and *dance* to help you with your research.

2. Get ready to set up a Mask Museum. Each group selects a mask. Draw it, trace it, or copy it. If you have a mask, bring it to class. Now, write a paragraph or two for museum visitors to read about your mask. Organize your ideas. First, write the name of the group or culture that uses it. Next, write the name of the mask or what it represents. Does it represent a **quality** (courage, love, anger, jealousy, etc.)? When do people wear the mask? Who wears the mask? Why do or did they wear it?

    Writing tip: Check your punctuation. Do you have a period, a question mark, or an exclamation mark at the end of each sentence? Capitalize proper nouns like *Greek*.

3. Make a mask to put in the museum. Draw, paint, or use collage techniques to create it.

4. Tour guides should be prepared to tell about the masks and answer questions. Visitors should be ready to ask questions about the masks.

    Listening/Speaking tip: Be sure you can pronounce the words you need to tell about the masks and the cultures they are from. Speak slowly and clearly. Use expression when you use words like *scary* to describe masks.

Check your progress:

Listening/Speaking: Tour guides: Did you speak clearly? Did visitors understand the descriptions you gave about the masks? Did they ask questions that showed they did?

Reading: Did you find the information you needed by reading reference materials?

Writing: Did you organize your information so that it was easily understood? Did you use capital letters with proper nouns? Did you punctuate sentences correctly?

Viewing: Did your masks help visitors understand what they represented? Did your masks help viewers understand more about the group or culture?

ODE TO MY SOCKS

Use with student text page 24.

Favorite Clothes Interview

1. Interview a partner about his or her favorite article of clothing. Ask your partner questions:

- *What is your favorite article of clothing?*
- *Would you please describe it?*
- *How did you get it?*
- *When do you wear it?*
- *Why do you like it so much?*

2. Share what your partner told you with a small group or the class.

3. Make a class tally and graph of which articles of clothing are the "favorite" of most classmates. Use the chart and graph sample below.

FAVORITE CLOTHES						
Article of Clothing:	*Shirt*	*Pants*	*Shoes*	*Hat*	_____	_____
Tally:						
Graph: (Fill in up to the total tallied.) 10 9 8 7 6 5 4 3 2 1						

Writing process. Have students use the **pre-writing strategy** of interviewing a partner and creating a class graph of their classmates' "favorite" clothes.

Use with student text page 30.

A Clothing Cluster Map

1. Look at an article of clothing very carefully and note all the details.
2. Write the name of the article of clothing in the large circle in the middle of the map.
3. Write two words that describe this article of clothing in the two connecting circles.
4. Write other words that connect ideas and clothing in the smallest circles.

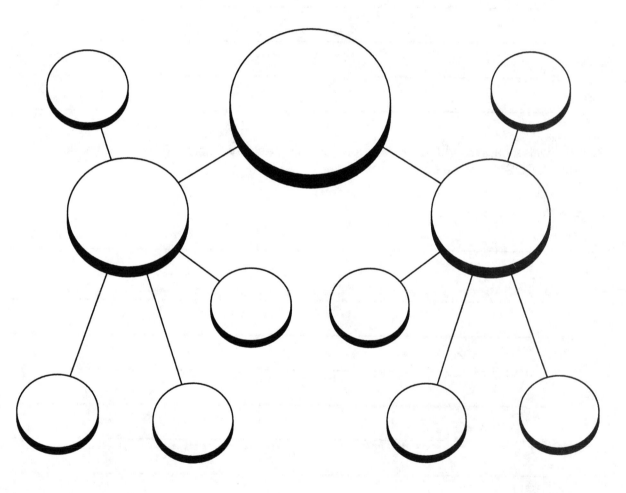

Writing process.   Students use the **pre-writing strategy** of a graphic organizer (cluster mapping) as they organize their ideas before writing an ode.

Use with student text page 31.

Writing an Ode

1. Use the words on your cluster map (Activity Master 12) and from Neruda's ode to write your own ode to your favorite article of clothing or object.

   Title: _____

   _____

   _____

   _____

   _____

   _____

   _____

2. Work with a partner and review your ode by using Activity Master 96 (Responding to Peers' Writing: EQS) found on page 123.

3. Rewrite your ode.

   Title: _____

   _____

   _____

   _____

   _____

   _____

   _____

4. Write your ode on a piece of paper or type it using a word processing program on a computer, and illustrate it with a drawing, painting, or photograph.

Listening/Speaking. **Writing purposes and evaluation.** Have students confer with each other and then read their completed odes aloud to their partners. Students write using the literary form of an ode and then work collaboratively evaluating their odes. **Enhancing the reading experience.** Have students listen to the selection on the cassette, then practice reading aloud. They should listen for pauses and exaggerated intonation for key words and practice this when reading aloud.

Use with student text pages 25–29.

A Gallery of Gifts: A Personal Narrative

Words to Know

enjoy   gift   give   holiday   present   received   surprise   use

Project Goal: In "Ode to My Socks," Pablo Neruda receives a pair of socks. The socks were a **gift,** or **present,** from a friend who made them. Have you **received** a gift that someone made for you? You will write about a gift you **gave** or received and talk to the class about it.

1. Look back at the poem "Ode to My Socks." Find words that Pablo Neruda used to describe the socks like "heavenly," "glowing," and "magnificent." How did Neruda feel about his gift? Then think of a gift you gave or received. What was it? How old were you when you received it? Was it a gift to keep and look at? Was it something to **use**? Was it a special trip or a party? Was it a **surprise**? Was the gift for a **holiday**? Did you **enjoy** the gift? Draw the gift.

    Reading tip: When you skim for information, it helps to look for key words. As you skim for words that describe the socks, look first for the words the poet uses to refer to the socks. Find words like "socks," "them," and "they."

    Pre-writing tip: List all of your ideas as you think of them. Then organize them in a cluster map like the one on Activity Master 12 on page 15. Write the name of the gift in the large circle. Then, list related details in the others. For example, write what you liked about it in one. In another, write how you feel about it today.

2. Write a story about the gift. Use "I" and tell what happened and how you felt about the gift. This kind of story is called a personal narrative.

    Writing tip: Read your story to a partner. Ask if the ideas are clear. Add more ideas and details. Use the editing checklists on pages 123 and 124.

3. If you still have the gift or a photo of it, bring it to class. Make a gallery of gifts in your classroom. Display each gift. Take turns telling about your gift and reading your stories aloud.

    Speaking tip: Practice your talk with a partner. Be sure you know how to say the words you want to use.

Extend: The next time you receive a gift, use some of these ideas to help you write a thank-you note. You could even write an ode as your way of saying thank you!

Check your progress:

Listening/Speaking: Did you practice your talk with a partner?

Reading: Did you skim for the word "socks" and other words the poet used for them? Did this help you find the words he used to describe them?

Writing: Did you use a cluster map to organize your ideas? Did you work with a partner to revise your writing?

Viewing: Did you include details in your drawing that helped others know what it was?

ACTIVITY 14 MASTER

Use with student text page 32.

Sunshine Outline

1. Did you or anyone you know ever get into trouble by borrowing something?

- Where were you?
- When did this happen?
- Who was with you?

- What did you borrow?
- What happened?
- How did you feel?

2. Write your answers next to the question words in the sun's rays.

3. Discuss your answers with your classmates.

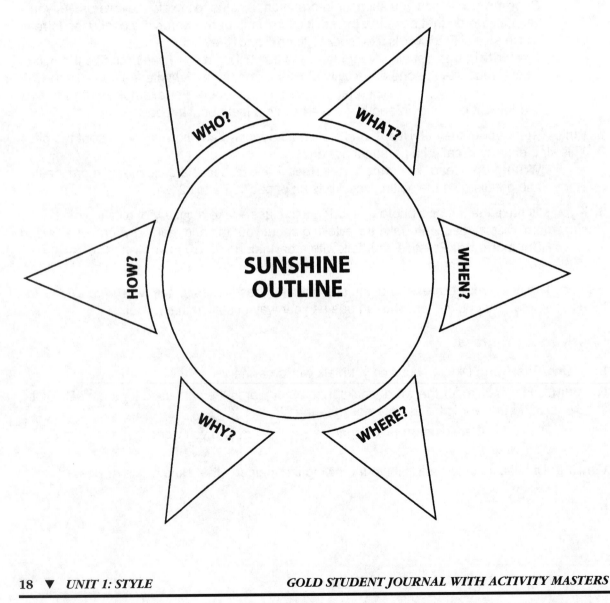

Writing process. Have students use the **pre-writing strategy** of a **graphic organizer** (sunshine outline) to generate ideas.

Use with student text page 46.

Character Development Chart

1. Choose a character from the story to analyze and study closely. Choose three qualities of that character to study. Some possible qualities are listed in the Key below.

2. Choose a line design from the Key to identify that quality and to show how this changes in the story.

3. Think about the character in the beginning of the story. Put a dot above "Beginning of Story" to indicate the amount of the quality (high or low) the character had at the beginning of the story. Do the same thing for the next two qualities.

4. Think about the character you have chosen in the middle and end of the story. Put a dot above "Middle of Story" and "End of Story" to indicate the amount of the quality the character had then.

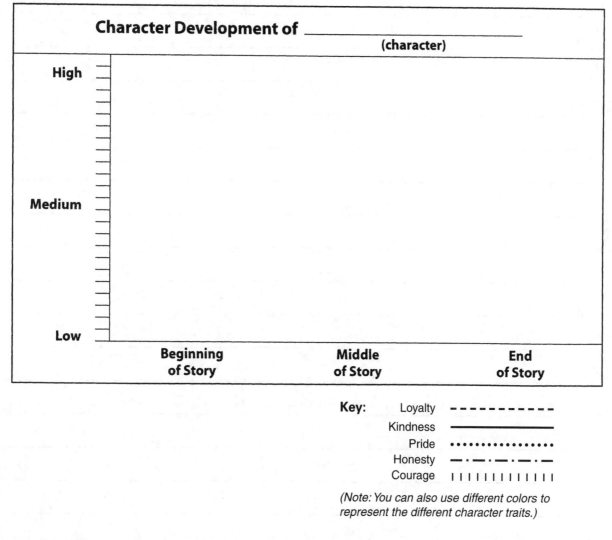

Character Development of _____
                                            (character)

High

Medium

Low

| Beginning of Story | Middle of Story | End of Story |

Key:

Loyalty	– – – – – – – –
Kindness	————————
Pride	••••••••••••••••
Honesty	—·—·—·—·—·
Courage	I I I I I I I I I I I I I

(Note: You can also use different colors to represent the different character traits.)

Listening/Speaking/evaluation. Students analyze the artistic element of character development.
Writing process and writing/inquiry/research. Students use the **pre-writing strategy** of a graphic organizer to create a chart to plan, develop, research, and analyze ideas of one character in "The Raiders Jacket."

Use with student text page 46.

ACTIVITY 16 MASTER

Writing About Character Change

1. How did the character you chose on Activity Master 15 change or develop in "The Raiders Jacket"? In what ways did the character stay the same? Use your character development chart to help you.

2. Write about your character. Describe how the character changed and how the events of the plot (the main events of the story) contributed to the development of that character. Use quotations from the text to support your ideas.

_____

_____

_____

_____

_____

_____

_____

_____

_____

_____

_____

_____

_____

_____

_____

_____

_____

_____

Listening/Speaking/evaluation. Students analyze the literary element of character development.

Writing/purpose. Have students choose a character and write a **reflective essay** on how the main events changed the character. Have them **edit,** making sure to use quotations and **quotation marks** to support their ideas.

Use with student text pages 33–43.

Tell Me about It!: A Teen Talk Show

Words to Know

conflict	problem	solve	talk it over	discuss	consequences
solution	decide	tell the truth	might	situation	unfair

Project Goal: In "The Raiders Jacket" a girl loses a friend's jacket. She must **decide** what to do. There are many **solutions**. She could **tell the truth**. She **might** pay her friend for the jacket. She might try to find it. She might **talk it over** with a friend. What would *you* do?

1. Form small groups. Choose one of these **situations** or write your own. Each one has a **conflict**, or **problem**, that you need to **solve**. For this project you will create a teen talk show.
   - You are very good at math. Your friend is sitting next to you during a math test. He or she wants to look at your answers. Will you let your friend look at your paper?
   - Your classmate invites you to a party at his or her house. Your parents don't know this classmate. They tell you that you can't go. You think they are **unfair**. How might you get them to change their minds?
   - Write your own situation. *Be sure you state a problem that has more than one solution.*
       Reading tip: If you don't understand a word or situation, ask your teacher for help, reread it with your group, or look in a dictionary.

2. **Discuss** two or three solutions and **consequences** to the situation.

3. Imagine that you are on TV on a teen talk show called *Tell Me about It!* One person in your group is the TV host and explains one of the problems above to the class. The other people in the group act out the problem for the audience. One person plays the role of a parent or older friend who gives advice. Another plays the role of "the teenager." The TV host invites the audience (the class) to ask questions and give another solution to the problem. If you can, videotape the talk show.
       Listening/Speaking tip: Be sure to use the right tone of voice when you are trying to convince someone that you are right.
       Viewing tip: Look at the gestures and facial expressions of the speakers. Did they help explain the problem?

Extend: Have fun making up and putting on other episodes of *Tell Me about It!*

Check your progress:

Listening/Speaking: Did the host explain the problem so that the audience understood it? Did the others act out their roles effectively?

Reading: Did you reread or ask for help about any situation you did not understand?

Writing: If you wrote your own situation, did you use a problem that has more than one solution?

Viewing: Audience: Did groups you watched use appropriate gestures? If you videotaped your own show, how do you rate your speaking and gestures?

Develop vocabulary and language for problem-solving with the Making Connections CD-ROM, Unit 7.

THE DRESS MESS

Use with student text page 48.

ACTIVITY 17 MASTER

Dress Code Interview

1. Interview three or four people who have attended more than one school.
2. Using the questions on the chart below, record their answers in the boxes.
3. Work with your classmates to make a class chart.

Name and location of school	Does the school have uniforms or other dress code?	What are the consequences of not following the code?	What is the effect of the dress code on your behavior and schoolwork?	What is the effect on other students' behavior and schoolwork?

Speaking/Listening. Have students work in small groups. Ask them to use the information they gathered to evaluate dress codes. As students collect their information, have them record it on the class chart (**graphic organizer**).

Uniforms Chart

1. Read the article about uniforms again. What is the main idea or *theme statement* from this article?

_____

_____

2. On the chart below, list the reasons why each group supports students wearing uniforms and reasons why each group is opposed to wearing uniforms. There may not be information for every box. Write the information you do find in the boxes below.

Group	Why are uniforms a good idea?	Why are uniforms not a good idea?
Elementary school students		
High school students		
Teachers		
Parents		
You		

Writing/process and **Writing/inquiry/research.**   Have students use the **pre-writing strategy** of a graphic organizer (Uniforms Chart) to inquire why uniforms are or are not a good idea. Then have them support their findings with examples on the chart above which becomes the basis for a five-paragraph persuasive essay.

THE DRESS MESS

Use with student text page 53.

Writing an Essay

1. Discuss your ideas about dress codes and uniforms with a small group of your classmates.

2. Using information from Activity Masters 17 and 18, your uniforms and dress codes charts, write a draft of your essay.

_____

_____

_____

_____

_____

_____

_____

_____

_____

_____

_____

_____

_____

_____

_____

_____

_____

3. Exchange essays with another student and use the Editing Checklist (Activity Master 97) to edit your essays. When your edited paper is returned, rewrite the essay, making the changes suggested by your classmate.

Writing/purpose: Persuasive. Have students write a five-paragraph **persuasive essay** either for or against dress codes. Include the three parts of an essay: introduction, body (three points with reasons and elaboration after each point), and a conclusion. Use the Editing Checklist on page 124 to check **punctuation**, **spelling**, **grammar, usage**, and **organization**.

Use with student text pages 49–51.

Read All about It!: A Newspaper Special Edition on Uniforms

Words to Know

editorial   interview   headline   edition   article   edit   editor

Project Goal: Use what you learned about uniforms from reading the article "The Dress Mess." Imagine that you work for a newspaper. Your job today is to write **articles**, with photographs, for a special **edition** about uniforms. Or you may choose to write an **editorial** or a letter to the **editor**.

1. Work in three small groups. First, decide together what each group will do.
   - One group will write an article about workers in the community who wear uniforms—police officers, crossing guards, nurses, or doctors. Choose a group to interview. Why is it important for these people to wear uniforms? Write an article about your interview.
   - Another group will write an article about sports teams and the uniforms they wear. Describe their uniforms. Do they wear helmets? Special shoes? Other protection?
   - Another group will write about school uniforms. Do schools in your community have uniforms? Write an editorial or a letter to the editor explaining why you want or don't want school uniforms.

2. To help you with your writing, do research. Conduct **interviews** and watch local TV shows. Read newspapers, look in books at the library, or find yearbooks at your school. Take photographs of people and the uniforms they wear. Don't forget to take notes!
   Speaking/Listening tip: For interviews, write out your questions first. Practice asking them, using the right tone of voice. Listen carefully for answers. Ask people to repeat if you don't understand.
   Writing tip: Arrange your ideas on a cluster map using Activity Master 12 on page 15.

3. Write a **headline** (title) for your article, editorial, or letter. Your headline should focus on your main idea. Write your first draft and **edit** it. Remember to keep your audience in mind as you write. Read your draft to a partner. Are your ideas clear? If possible, use a computer to produce your final draft.

4. With the other groups, lay out your newspaper. How will you arrange the articles? Where will you put the photos? How many pages will you have? Display your newspaper for others to read.
   Viewing tip: Look at local or school papers. How do the articles appear on the page?

Extend: Follow a similar procedure for other topics that interest you in *Voices in Literature*.

Check your progress:

Listening/Speaking: Did the interview questions you asked get the answers you needed?
Reading: Did you give the main idea of your article, letter, or editorial in your headline?
Writing: Did you express your ideas clearly? Did you write for your audience?
Viewing: Did you look for pictures in newspapers or on TV?

Learn more clothing words with The Newbury House Dictionary CD-ROM, Unit 22. Develop vocabulary and language about clothing with the Making Connections CD-ROM, Unit 4.

ACTIVITY 20 MASTER

Write a Persuasive Letter

Words to Use

think	should	believe	for	reason	furthermore
feel	must	opinion	against	for example	in addition

Goal: Write a persuasive letter, using the prompt, or writing assignment, below. Follow each step.

1. Read the prompt, or writing assignment. What will you be writing about? Who is your audience? Focus on the purpose of your writing: to persuade.

Prompt: In some schools, students must wear uniforms. The principal of your school wants to require uniforms at your school. What is your position on this issue? Write a letter to the principal stating your position, or point of view. Support your point of view with convincing reasons. Be sure to explain your reasons.

2. To help you decide which position you will take, make a chart like this one on which you will list reasons FOR and reasons AGAINST the idea:

FOR	AGAINST
Easy to decide what to wear	Can't wear what you want to
No one dresses better than anyone else	Takes away freedom

3. Now that you have decided on a position, complete an organizer like this one for your main ideas, or reasons. List three details for each main idea:

Main Idea #1	Main Idea #2	Main Idea #3

4. Write a draft of your letter. Use five paragraphs and indent each one. Try to have five sentences in paragraphs 2, 3, and 4. Use words from Words to Use. See Activity Master 59, on page 75, to help you set up your letter.

Paragraph 1: Introduce yourself and state your position.
Paragraph 2: State one reason and explain it.
Paragraph 3: State another reason and explain it.
Paragraph 4: State your third reason and explain it.
Paragraph 5: Summarize your three main ideas or reasons. Use your last sentence to persuade the reader to agree with you.

Work with a partner and give each other feedback. Be sure to tell one thing you liked and one way your partner could improve the letter. Use the checklists on pages 123 and 124.

5. Write your final draft. Read your drafts aloud. Compare your views with your classmates'.

Writing/purpose: personal. Ask students to write about a topic that has high interest to them. As a guideline, have them write in a style and voice appropriate for the audience who will read their work.
Silent Reading. Have students use the readings suggested on page 55 of the student text during Sustained Silent Reading Periods. Encourage students to use appropriate reading strategies to monitor their comprehension.

Use with student text page 58.

Wedding and Marriage Customs

1. Interview your parents or grandparents, and ask them to describe their wedding. Record their responses on the chart below.

2. Make a chart of the marriage customs from your country or region by combining the information on your chart with the information that other students from your country collected.

Interview Questions	Answers
Who decides who will marry?	
How do people get ready for the wedding?	
Who pays for what?	
What are the wedding ceremonies like?	
What kinds of parties are held?	
Where do the bride and groom live afterward?	
How old are the bride and groom usually?	

UNIT 2: SUSPENSE

Listening/Speaking/critical listening. Have students interview family members and actively listen to record their responses.

Writing/inquiry/research. Encourage students to compile their results into the customs chart or use a computer to create a chart. Finally, ask them to **summarize** the results from their research and share them with the class.

Use with student text page 66.

Culture Map

1. Reread "The Ghost's Bride" to answer the questions below. Not all the questions are easy to answer from information in the story. Sometimes you must guess, or *infer*, the answer.
2. Work with a partner to answer as many questions as you can.
3. Compare your answers with your classmates' answers.

Question	Answer
What is the name of the culture?	
Where do the people live?	
What is the land like?	
What is the climate like?	
Who lives together?	
How do people make a living?	
How does the group practice religion?	
How do people stay healthy?	
Who are the leaders? How do people make decisions?	

Reading/comprehension/study strategies. Have students read "The Ghost's Bride" to discover the answers to the questions above, using the Culture Map chart for **study guide questions**.

Writing process: pre-writing strategy. Students can use the chart to organize their ideas before writing a suspense story.

Use with student text page 67.

ACTIVITY 23 MASTER

Suspense Stories

1. Share stories of suspense with a small group of students.
2. Make a culture map (Activity Master 22) of your story or of one of the stories you heard.
3. Write a suspense story below. Be sure to include the elements of culture that are on your culture map.

_____

_____

_____

_____

_____

_____

_____

_____

_____

_____

_____

_____

_____

_____

_____

_____

_____

_____

UNIT 2: SUSPENSE

Reading/Comprehension.   Encourage students to draw on their own cultural background as they share suspense stories.
Writing/purpose: personal response to literature.   Have students write a suspense story using elements of culture from the Culture Map on the previous page.

Lights, Camera, Action: A Reader's Theater Production

Words to Know

scene	narrator	dialogue	props
setting	characters	costumes	Reader's Theater

Project Goal: Have you ever wanted to be on stage? Here's your chance. You and your classmates will create and perform a **Reader's Theater** performance of "The Ghost's Bride." In a Reader's Theater, you use your own words and act out what happens.

1. Your teacher will divide "The Ghost's Bride" into **scenes**. Work in small groups. Each group will write a scene in their own words and then perform it.

2. Write your scene in the form of a play. One person in your group will be the **narrator** and the others will be **characters** (for example, the mother and the daughter). The narrator will tell the story and the characters will say the **dialogue**, or the speakers' actual words. You can use dialogue from the play and make up some new dialogue.
   Writing tip: In a play, capitalize the character's name and follow it with a colon.
   Mother: Come back right away.
   Daughter: I will.

3. In your group, practice performing your scene. Give each other suggestions for improving your performance. Here are some examples: *Carlos, maybe you could speak more slowly. Ling, try to use more gestures.*

4. In your group, draw a large poster that shows the **setting** of your scene (for example, the stream and the rock on which the girl rested). You can also bring in **props** and **costumes** to help make your performance exciting.
   Reading tip: Reread your scene to find descriptions of the setting. Try to include the details of the description in your drawing.

5. Each group performs its scene for the class. When the narrator is reading, the characters will act out the story with gestures.
   Speaking tip: As you perform, use gestures and change your voice to show emotion.

Extend: Write and perform an original play for your classmates.

Check your progress:

Listening/Speaking: Did you use gestures? Did you change your voice to show emotion?
Reading: Did you reread your scene to help you draw the setting?
Writing: Did you capitalize each character's name and use a colon after it?
Viewing: Did you add props and costumes to make your performance exciting and understandable?

Use with student text page 72.

Word Pairs and Patterns

1. With a partner, look at the poem "hist whist" again, and find as many pairs of related words as you can.

2. Write them on the chart below. An example is given in the first row.

First Word	Second Word	Changes
twitchy	*witches*	• *t* dropped from the beginning of *twitchy* • *y* changed to *es* in *witches*

UNIT 2: SUSPENSE

Listening/Speaking/critical listening.   Have partners take turns reading aloud the poem "hist whist" and **actively listening** for the effect of the related words they have listed. Students should **distinguish and produce sounds** found in word pairs and patterns, and then record their results on the chart above.

Use with student text page 72.

Sound Devices in Poetry

1. Look in Appendix B of the student text, "Guide to Literary Terms and Techniques," pages 242–247, and write the definitions for *repetition, alliteration, assonance,* and *parallelism* in the boxes next to each word.

2. Look through the selections you have read and find examples of each sound device. Write these in the "examples" boxes.

3. Make a class chart of all the sound devices you have found.

Name of Device	Definition	Examples
Repetition		
Alliteration		
Assonance		
Parallelism		

Listening/Speaking/critical listening. In pairs, have students take turns reading the examples aloud while listening and distinguishing the effects of each sound-pattern device.

Writing/purposes and inquiry. Students use this graphic organizer as a **pre-writing strategy** for the activity on page 33.

Use with student text page 73.

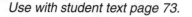

ACTIVITY 26 MASTER

Free Verse Poem

UNIT 2: SUSPENSE

1. Think about the last time you were scared or in suspense.

2. Write two stanzas in free verse. In free verse, the poet does not use rhyming words or a set rhythm. This type of poem makes poetry sound more like speech.

3. In the first stanza, use sounds to set the mood of the poem. Use some of the words you wrote on your word pairs and patterns chart (Activity Master 24).

_____

_____

_____

_____

_____

4. In the second stanza, offer the reader a warning and tell the reader why.

_____

_____

_____

_____

_____

5. In a small group, review your poem, using Activity Master 96 (Responding to Peers' Writing: EQS), and rewrite it, using the suggestions you receive from other classmates. Use a separate piece of paper.

Writing/purpose: literary and form.   Encourage students to personally respond to the suspense reading by writing in a free verse style using sounds, word pairs, and patterns.

Listening/Speaking/evaluation.   Ask students to use Activity Master 96 (Responding to Peers' Writing: EQS) page 123, to receive feedback suggestions from their peers.

Sounds Real, Real Sounds:
An Audio/Visual Poem

Words to Know

audio/visual   language   record   sound   tape recorder

Project Goal: In the poem "hist whist," the poet plays with **language** and **sound**. For your project, you will tape-record sounds around your school. You and your group will use sounds, pictures, and words to make an **audio/visual** poem.

Work in small groups. You will need a **tape recorder**. Each person needs a notebook and pen.

1. First, choose a place in the school or community where you want to **record** sounds. Choose a place with a lot of activity: the cafeteria, a sports game after school, the hallway between classes, or another busy place. Before you start recording, listen to the sounds in the place. Make a list of sounds you want to record.

2. Record three minutes of sounds. You may start and stop the tape. Include people speaking, machines, footsteps, yelling, or anything that you usually hear in that place. Take turns using the tape recorder.

3. Next, observe the place. Write a list of things you see. Listen for words or phrases you hear people say. Write them in your notebook.
   Writing tip: Don't write complete sentences. Take notes writing several words about what you see and hear, such as: *a long, long line, "Meet me there!," lockers slamming.*

4. With your group, read the words and phrases you wrote. Choose some of the words and phrases from each person's list and form them into a poem. Use the poem "hist whist" in your student text as a model. Don't write in complete sentences. Write your group's poem on a poster. Decorate the poster with drawings and photos or other things you can glue on.
   Writing tip: Be sure to include adjectives. Use interesting adverbs.

5. Present your audio/visual poem to the class. Read your poem and use your tape recording as background. Use feeling and emotion as you speak to show listeners what this place is like.

Check your progress:

Listening/Speaking: Did you use an appropriate tone of voice and speak with emotion when you presented your poem?

Reading: Did you reread "hist whist" and use it to help you write your own poem?

Writing: Did you use idioms or informal language? Did you write for a student audience?

Viewing: Did you decorate your poster with drawings or objects from the place you observed?

Use with student text page 80.

Character Web

1. Choose a character from the story and write that person's name in the middle of the character web below.

2. Label each of the four boxes with a descriptive word about the character (e.g., *beautiful, wise, mysterious*).

3. Write words in each box that support your description. You can use the wise woman's own words and actions, the narrator's words, and your own ideas from your reading of the text.

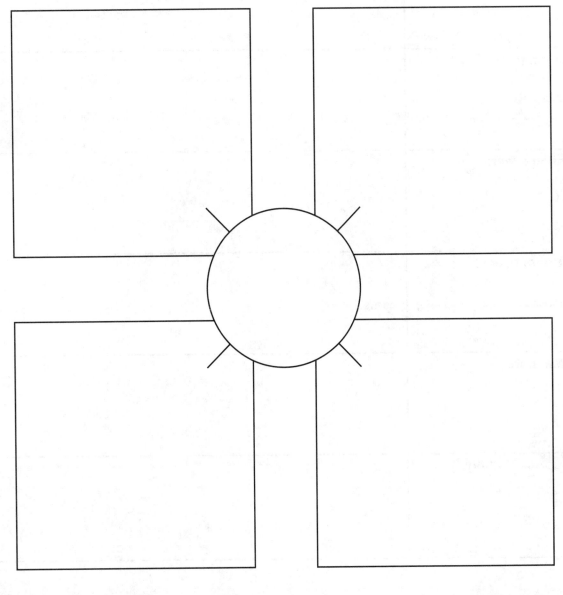

UNIT 2: SUSPENSE

Writing process: pre-writing strategy. Have students use this graphic organizer (Character Web) to list descriptive words, with supportive details, about the character.

Use with student text page 81.

Folktale Story Map

1. Think about a folktale you have heard your family tell.
2. Use the folktale story map to outline the main elements of your folktale.

Title: _____	
Story Elements	
Characters:	
Setting:	
Initial event:	
Turn of events:	
Reaction:	
Suprise Ending:	

Writing process: pre-writing strategy. Have students use this graphic organizer (Folktale Story Map) to outline the main story elements such as character, setting, initial event, etc., in order to develop a narrative draft outline for writing a folktale.

UNIT 2: SUSPENSE

Use with student text page 81.

ACTIVITY 29 MASTER

Writing a Folktale

1. Use your folktale story map and character web to write a folktale. Be sure to put lots of detail in your folktale. Help your readers see your characters and places through your words.

2. If you choose a tale of suspense, try to include foreshadowing. *Foreshadowing* gives readers a clue or hint about events that have not yet happened in the story. Use foreshadowing to create a feeling of suspense or surprise in the reader.

3. Ask a classmate to use Activity Master 96 (Responding to Peers' Writing: EQS), on page 123, to provide comments on your folktale.

UNIT 2: SUSPENSE

Writing/purpose: Personal response to literature.   Have each student create his or her own folktale using **foreshadowing**.
Writing/evaluation.   Have peers respond to each other's folktales using Activity Master 96 (page 123).

Use with student text pages 75–79.

"The Disappearance of...": Write and Perform an Original Mystery Story

Words to Know

| eerie | scary | plot | howling | moan | foreshadowing |
| suspenseful | afraid | suprise | mysterious | setting | sound effects |

Project Goal: "The Wise Woman of Córdoba" is a mystery story. What makes it **suspenseful**? For this project, you will write your own mystery story and present it to the class, using **sound effects** (noises), illustrations, and costumes.

1. Like most stories, mystery stories have a beginning, middle, and end. The *beginning* of mystery stories often uses **foreshadowing**. The *middle* has the action, and the *ending* often has a **surprise**. Think of ideas and a **plot** for a mystery story with the title: *"The Disappearance of...."* What kind of characters will you have? What is the **setting**? Will it take place in the past, present, or future?

   Writing tip: List all of your ideas as you think of them. Then organize them using a story map (see Activity Master 28, page 36). Do you have a beginning, a middle, and an unexpected ending?

2. Now write a draft of the story. Use words from the mystery stories you read and from the "Words to Know" section at the top of this page, like *scary, afraid, howling, moan,* and *mysterious*. When you are finished, work with a partner for ideas on improving your story. Write a final draft. Illustrate your story with pictures you draw or ones from magazines. Prepare sound effects like **eerie** music.

   Writing tip: Read your story to a partner. Ask him or her if the ideas are clear. Add more details. Use the editing checklists on pages 123 and 124.

3. Practice reading your story with a partner. Use gestures and change your voice to add to the suspense of the story. As you read, your partner can make sound effects. Or, you can prepare the sound effects on a tape and play the tape during your performance. Decide on a costume you will wear and how will you use your illustrations to add to the suspense.

4. Now read your story to the class or a smaller group. Use your gestures, voice, costume, and illustrations to make the story come alive.

Check your progress:

Listening/Speaking: Did you use gestures and sound effects as you read your story?
Reading: Did you include foreshadowing and adjectives like the ones found in the mystery stories you read?
Writing: Did you use a story map to organize your ideas? Did you work with a partner to revise your writing?
Viewing: Did your costume and props help others visualize your ideas better and make the story more suspenseful and scary?

Use with student text page 82.

Two-Column Chart

1. Think about an unbelievable story that you have heard.
2. Use the chart below to write your ideas about what makes you want to believe an unbelievable story and what makes you not want to believe (doubt) an unbelievable story.
3. Share your ideas with your class and make a class chart.

Why I want to believe the story	Why I doubt the story

UNIT 2: SUSPENSE

Listening/Speaking.   Have students choose valid evidence or proofs to support claims about what makes a believable versus doubtful story, and share their ideas with classmates.

Writing process: pre-writing strategy.   Have students use this graphic organizer (Two-Column Chart) to support their claims.

Use with student text page 86.

ACTIVITY **31** MASTER

UNIT 2: SUSPENSE

Comparing and Contrasting
Two Versions of a Story

1. In the left-hand circle, write details and events from the North Carolina version of "The Hitchhiker."
2. In the right-hand circle, write details and events from the Korean version of the story.
3. In the middle, where the two circles overlap, write details and events that are in both versions of the story.

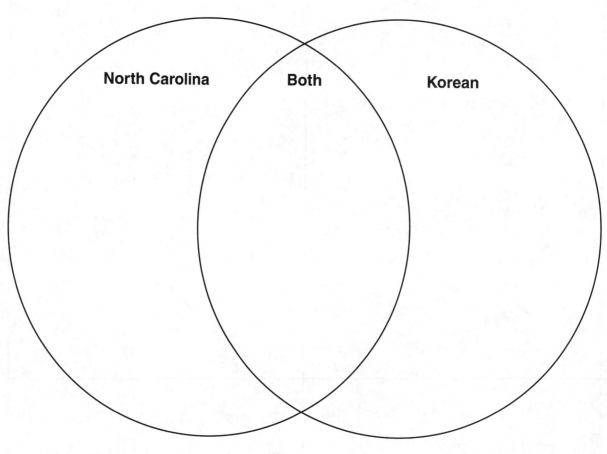

North Carolina   Both   Korean

Writing process: pre-writing strategy. Have students use the above graphic organizer (Venn diagram) to analyze, compare, and contrast two versions of a story.

Use with student text page 87.

Anecdotes

An *anecdote* is a brief account of an interesting event in someone's life. Anecdotes are often used to make a point, describe a person, or explain an idea, and they can be humorous or serious.

1. Write an anecdote about yourself. Tell about something that happened to you. Explain why it happened or why it was an important event in your life.

_____

_____

_____

_____

_____

_____

_____

2. In a small group, read your anecdote to the other students. Listen while the other students read their anecdotes to you. List all points, ideas, or personal traits you hear.

_____

_____

_____

_____

_____

_____

Writing/purpose: personal form/autobiographical anecdote.   Have students write an anecdote about themselves.

Listening/Speaking/critical listening.   Have students listen to classmates' anecdotes and list points, ideas, and personal traits.

UNIT 2: SUSPENSE

Use with student text pages 83–85.

Getting from Here to There: A Visitor's Guide

Words to Know

transportation	bus	arrive	schedule
visitor's guide	depart	index	map

Project Goal: Every day, people need to get from one place to another. Doing this is not usually as strange as it was in "The Hitchhiker." Help yourself and others get around by researching and writing a **Visitor's Guide** to your community or one close by. Where do people need or want to go? What kind of **transportation** can help them get there? What are some fun places?

1. As a class, make a list of places in the community you often go in a chart like the one below.

Place	Activity	Directions	Hours	Cost
Royal Cinema	Watch movies	Take bus #22 to Park St.	4:30–midnight	$4.50

2. Each of you should pick one place and do some research. Find directions, hours, and cost of admission or services for the place. Can people get there by car, **bus**, train, bike, or foot? Locate schedules and information. Work with a partner to read a bus or train **schedule**. Find words like *arrive* and *depart* to help you. Use a **map** to locate your place.
    Reading tip: Use the yellow pages of the phone book or the Internet to gather information. You may need to try several key words to find the places you want. In the phone book, city offices and buildings are under *government numbers* in the **index**.

3. Write a short description of your place. Include directions, hours, costs, and a short explanation of why this is a good place to visit. Revise and publish your paragraph using the checklists on pages 123–124. If you have a computer, write your description in a word processing program.
    Writing tip: Think about your audience. What will people want to know about each place?

4. Find brochures and ads. Take photos. Create a Visitor's Guide with the pictures, map, and the description you wrote. Tell the class or a small group about the place.
    Speaking/Listening tip: Use description in your talk.

Check your progress:

Listening/Speaking: Did you use your description to help you give your talk?

Reading: Did you read schedules carefully to get the correct information?

Writing: Did you consider your audience when you wrote about the places in your community?

Viewing: Did you notice differences in ads and brochures about the place you researched?

Learn vocabulary about going places with The Newbury House Dictionary CD-ROM, Unit 12. Develop vocabulary and language about travel with the Making Connections CD-ROM, Unit 6.

Use with student text page 88.

Cluster Map

1. Do you know any stories about people who turn into animals? What kind of animals are in the stories?
2. Write the name of an animal in the large circle in the middle of this cluster map.
3. Write two words that describe this animal in the two smaller connecting circles.
4. Write other ideas and words in the smallest circles.

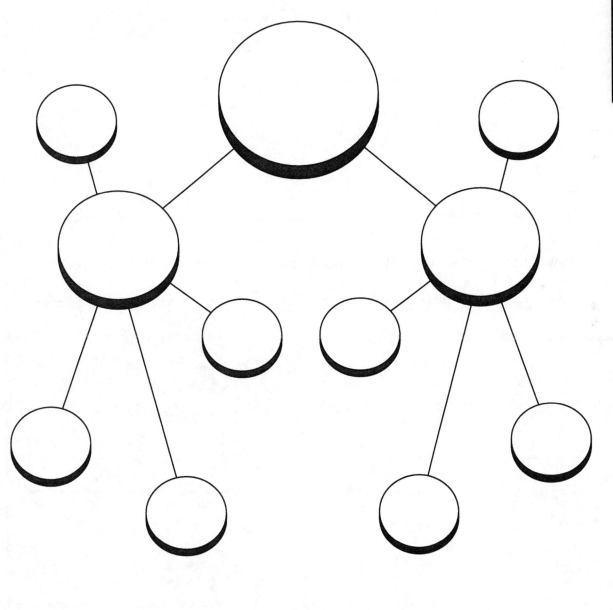

Writing process: pre-writing strategy.   Have students use the above graphic organizer to brainstorm ideas and words that they can use to write a story.

Use with student text page 96.

Draw the Setting

1. Draw a picture of the home as you imagined it *before* you knew who the wife and husband were.

2. Draw a picture of the home as you imagined it *after* you found out who the wife and husband were.

Second language writing. Encourage students to draw pictures as a pre-writing activity to compare and contrast the *before* and *after* settings they imagined.

Use with student text page 97.

Writing from Another Point of View

1. The following example is the beginning of "The Wife's Story." It is told from the sister's point of view:

   My sister had a good husband, a good father for her children, we thought. She doesn't understand what happened, but I was always suspicious. He seemed gentle. When I saw him playing with the children, he looked as if there wasn't any bad in him, not one mean bone….

2. Retell "The Wife's Story" from the point of view of a different person. It could be told from the point of view of another character (first person), by a narrator (omniscient point of view), or a third person (limited third person).

_____

_____

_____

_____

_____

_____

_____

_____

_____

_____

_____

_____

_____

_____

_____

UNIT 2: SUSPENSE

Writing/purpose: literary.   Have students respond to literature by writing from a different literary point of view: for example, first person, omniscient point of view (narrator), or third person.

Use with student text pages 89–95.

Tonight's Top Story—Man or Wolf?: A Newscast

Words to Know

newscast   point of view   reporter   interview   eye contact

Project Goal: You are going to create and perform a television **newscast** about the events in "The Wife's Story." You and your classmates will play the roles of the **reporter**, the wife, the wife's sister, and the daughter. Work in groups of four.

1. To make a good news story, reporters ask questions. Use the Sunshine Outline (Activity Master 14, page 18) to list the reporter's "Wh" questions: Who? What? When? Where? Why? How?

2. Decide who will play the roles of each character. The characters must answer the questions from their **points of view**. For point of view ideas, skim the text to find where the wife, her sister, and the daughter are mentioned in the story.
   Reading tip: As you skim for the wife's reactions, look for the words that show her feelings, like "the awful thing," "don't believe in it," and "brings the shivers on me."

3. Write the reporter's introduction to the news story, one that will get the attention of the audience. Tell a) who the reporter is, b) where he or she is, c) what the story is about, and d) whom he or she is interviewing.
   Example: I'm Lena Martinez, coming to you from The Forest, where a wolf has turned into a man! I'm talking to the wolf's wife, the wife's sister, and the wolf's daughter.
   Writing tip: Brainstorm ways that the reporter can get the viewer's attention, while at the same time giving information.

4. Perform your newscast for the class and videotape it, if possible. Afterwards, have the audience tell important events and ideas learned from the videotaped performance.
   Listening/Speaking tip: The reporter and the person being interviewed should make **eye contact** with the person he or she is talking to.

Extend: Watch the local TV news. Take notes on an **interview**. How many of the "Wh" questions do the reporters ask?

Check your progress:

Listening/Speaking: Did you make eye contact with the person you were talking to?

Reading: Did you get the information you needed when you skimmed the story?

Writing: Did you use words in your introduction that would get the attention of your audience?

Viewing: When you viewed your newscast, was its purpose clear? Was all the key information included?

UNIT 2: SUSPENSE

Use with student text page 98.

Word Round Table

1. List as many words as you can to express sadness. Use translation and English-English dictionaries and a thesaurus to help you make your list.

_____

_____

_____

_____

_____

_____

_____

2. In a small group, share your list with other students. Add words that you do not have.

3. Write sentences that contain the words from your word list. Try to write sentences that contain more than one of the words. For example:

The unhappy man was distraught and sad after his daughter died.

_____

_____

_____

_____

_____

_____

_____

_____

Reading/word identification/vocabulary development: Have students use a dictionary and thesaurus to make a list of words that mean the same as *sadness*.

Writing/inquiry/research. Students are asked to use writing as a study tool to refer to and use information.

UNIT 2: SUSPENSE

Paraphrasing the Poem

1. Choose a stanza of "The Raven" and copy it below.

_____

_____

_____

_____

_____

_____

2. Rewrite the stanza in your own words. If you don't understand a word, look it up in your dictionary.

_____

_____

_____

_____

_____

_____

_____

_____

_____

_____

_____

_____

_____

3. Read your rewritten stanza to the class. Then, as a group, read your rewritten stanzas, following the order the stanzas appear in the poem.

Reading/word identification/vocabulary development: Have students use a dictionary as a reference for unknown words.
Writing/purposes: personal. Have students personally respond to literature by paraphrasing a stanza of a poem.

ACTIVITY 38 MASTER

Rhyme Scheme

1. Find the rhyming words at the end of each line in the first stanza of the poem "The Raven"— for example, *dreary* and *weary*.
2. Draw a line under each rhyming word you find.
3. Label each set of rhyming words with a letter, starting with "a," then "b," then "c." For example, the words *dreary* and *weary* should both have an "a" above them. Put a "b" above the next set of rhyming words in the stanza, and so on. Begin again with the letter "a" when you start the second stanza.

UNIT 2: SUSPENSE

Stanza 1	Stanza 2

Once upon a midnight dreary,
    while I pondered, weak and weary,
Over many a quaint and curious
    volume of forgotten lore,—
While I nodded, nearly napping,
    suddenly there came a tapping,
As of someone gently rapping,
    rapping at my chamber door.
"'Tis some visitor," I muttered,
    "tapping at my chamber door,—
Only this and nothing more."
	Ah, distinctly I remember
	    it was in the bleak December,
	And each separate dying ember
	    wrought its ghost upon the floor.
	Eagerly I wished the morrow;—
	    vainly I had sought to borrow
	From my books surcease of sorrow,—
	    sorrow for the lost Lenore—
	For the rare and radiant maiden whom
	    the angels name Lenore—
	Nameless *here* for evermore.

4. What is the pattern of each stanza?

STANZA 1: _____

STANZA 2: _____

5. On a separate piece of paper, write out the words of your favorite song. Underline the last word of each sentence or phrase. What is the rhyme scheme of that song?

Listening/Speaking/critical listening. Have students work with partners and take turns reading aloud the stanzas and the words of their favorite songs. Have partners **actively listen** for the pattern of rhyming words. Have students write out the words of their favorite song and **use the written song to discover** the rhyme scheme.

Use with student text page 107.

Writing about Poetry

Write a short composition about "The Raven" or another poem of your choice. Include the following:

- What the poem is about
- What mood the poem expresses
- What poetic devices, such as assonance, rhyme, and repetition, the poet uses
- Your response to the poem
- How the rhyme scheme fits the mood of the poem

UNIT 2: SUSPENSE

_____

_____

_____

_____

_____

_____

_____

_____

_____

_____

_____

_____

_____

_____

_____

_____

_____

_____

Listening/Speaking/critical listening. Encourage students to take turns reading aloud the poetic devices the poet used. Have classmates **actively listen and tell** what effect these devices have.

Writing/inquiry/evaluation. Have students write about poetic devices such as rhyme and repetition used in "The Raven."

Use with student text pages 99–105.

Animals as Symbols: A Research Project

Words to Know

symbols symbolize represent reminds (someone) of

Project Goal: Animals are often used as **symbols** in literature. Ravens **symbolize,** or **represent**, death in Edgar Allen Poe's poem "The Raven." Why? The raven is black, a color that symbolizes death in some cultures. Ravens make a loud, crying sound that **reminds** people **of** human cries. For this project, think about an animal that symbolizes a state or quality and write about it.

1. Choose one of these qualities or states or list one of your own. Look up the word in a dictionary.

   freedom   peace   jealousy   power   greed   love
   friendship   bravery   anger   loyalty   happiness   pride

2. Choose an animal that you think symbolizes this state or quality. For example, you might choose a dog to symbolize loyalty. Use a cluster map to organize some ideas about your animal. Put your animal in the center of the cluster and write your thoughts around it.

3. Write a paragraph about your animal. Explain why it symbolizes the quality or state.

4. Research your animal on the Internet or in an encyclopedia. Find some scientific facts about your animal. Is there a reason why your animal seems to symbolize the quality? Here's an example. Perhaps you wrote that a lion symbolizes bravery. You find out that lions don't have many enemies and don't run away from other animals. They seem "brave." Write a second paragraph and add these scientific facts. Do the scientific facts support your ideas or not? Revise your report after reading it to a partner.
   Writing tip: Be sure to read your report to a partner. Ask him or her if your ideas are clear. Read your partner's report and give him or her suggestions for revising it.

Check your progress:

Listening/Speaking: Did you ask your partner if your ideas were clear?

Reading: Did you use reference materials to find information? (dictionary, thesaurus, Internet, encyclopedia)

Writing: Did you develop your ideas in the first paragraph? Did you use scientific facts in the second paragraph? Did you read your writing to a partner and revise it?

UNIT 2: SUSPENSE

Write a Reflective Essay: A Response to Literature

Words to Use

think	recommend	suspense	first of all
feel	opinion	suspenseful	in conclusion

Goal: You are going to write a reflective essay using the prompt, or writing assignment, below.

1. Read the prompt, or writing assignment. What will you be writing about? Who is your audience? Focus on the purpose of your writing: to share your thoughts.

Prompt: You have just read a unit with suspense stories. Your local newspaper is going to feature suspense stories. They have asked you to recommend one to include. Decide which story was the most suspenseful. Write an essay telling why this story should be included. Include details about what made it so suspenseful.

2. Decide on the story you will recommend. Use a word web to list what made the story suspenseful. Write adjectives and phrases in each large circle and details on the lines.

SCARY   DIDN'T KNOW WHAT WOULD HAPPEN NEXT   SURPRISE ENDING

3. List your main ideas with three suporting reasons in the order that you will present them.

Main Idea #1:	Main Idea #2:	Main Idea #3:

4. Write your draft. Use five paragraphs and indent each one. Try to have five sentences in each paragraph. Use words from the Words to Use list above.

Paragraph 1: State your recommendation.

Paragraph 2: State one reason and explain it.

Paragraph 3: State another reason and explain it.

Paragraph 4: State your third reason and explain it.

Paragraph 5: Summarize your three main ideas or reasons. Use your last sentence to convince the newspaper editor why this story would be a good choice.

Work with a partner and give each other feedback. Be sure to tell one thing you like and one way your partner could improve the letter. Use the checklists on pages 123–124.

5. Write your final draft. Read and compare your views with others in the class.

Use with student text page 112.

Concentric Circles

1. Where do you live? Use the circles below. Begin with the word "Universe" and write a new place in each circle. As you move toward the center of the circle, each place should be smaller and more specific.
2. Next to each word, write something or someone important to you in that place.

UNIT 3: LOVE

Writing process: pre-writing strategy.   Have students use the graphic organizer (Concentric Circles) to organize their ideas before they write.

Use with student text page 114.

Walking Gallery of Imagery

1. As you read the poem "Although I Conquer All the Earth," use your imagination to create images or pictures in your mind about the poem.

2. Draw some of those pictures or images below.

3. Share your images with a small group of students. On a large piece of paper, combine your images with the images by other students.

4. Post your group picture on the wall along with the pictures from other groups. One student from each group should stand by the group picture and be ready to answer questions about the images there.

5. Walk around and ask questions about the pictures. Make notes below.

_____

_____

_____

_____

_____

UNIT 3: LOVE

Listening/Speaking/purpose. Have students display their artwork in response to the poem they just read. As they **view** the art, have them ask questions about the pictures.

Use with student text page 115.

Using Parallel Structures

1. Think about someone or something important to you. Where is this person or object? Use the concentric circles below. You can start far away and come closer, as the poet in "Although I Conquer All the Earth" does, or you can start up close and move farther away with each line.

2. In the poem "Although I Conquer All the Earth," the poet uses the parallel structure "In that_____, there is only one_____." Think about a parallel structure to describe where your person or object is. Write that structure in the concentric circles below with each place. Use the places you listed on Activity Master 41 to help you.

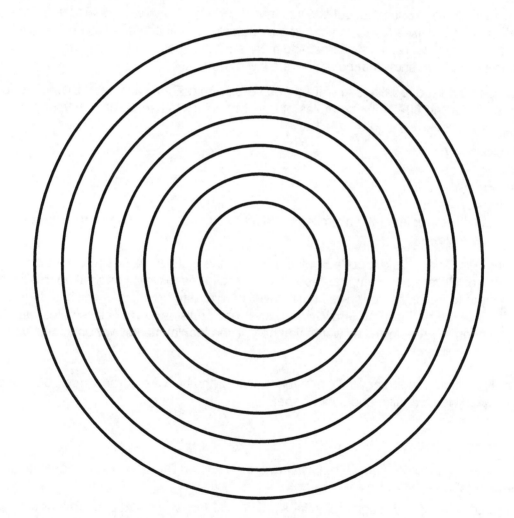

3. Write a draft poem about your object or person, using the parallel structure you wrote on the circles above. When you finish, read your draft poem to a classmate and ask him or her to respond to your poem.

Writing process: pre-writing strategy.   Have students use the graphic organizer (Concentric Circles) to organize their ideas before they write.

Writing/conventions.   Have students write using **parallelism** to describe a person or object.

UNIT 3: LOVE

Use with student text page 113.

The Ideal Friend: A Free Verse Poem

Words to Know

like   as   ideal   simile   collage   free verse

Project Goal: In the poem "Although I Conquer All the Earth," the poet shows how important one woman is. People, especially good friends, make a difference in our lives. What qualities make a good friend? In this project, you will write a **free verse** poem about your **ideal** friend.

1. Brainstorm qualities that describe your ideal friend. Is it someone who likes to be with family, helps others, or plays sports? Use a cluster map to help you organize your ideas.

2. Skim through magazines. Cut out pictures that show a quality of your ideal friend. For example, if your ideal friend likes to fish, you could cut out a picture of someone fishing. You can also choose pictures that represent something more abstract about your friend—for example, a picture of a cake to show that he or she is a sweet person.

3. Now use your list of qualities to write a free verse poem about your friend. (See student text pages 25–29 and 69–71 for examples of free verse.) Try to use **similes** in your poem.

   Example:

   My ideal friend
   Is sweet.
   She swims like a fish
   And gets up early.

   > **Writing tip:** To make a simile, compare two things using **like** or **as.** ("She's as funny as a clown.")

4. On another paper, make a **collage** of your magazine pictures to illustrate your poem. You can also draw your own pictures. Tape all of the collages to a wall or chalkboard. Then read your poem to the class. Your classmates will listen, and try to identify which collage is yours.

   > **Speaking/Listening and Viewing tips:** As you listen to your classmates read their poems, write down key words you hear. Then look at the key words to help you identify the collages.

Extend: Next time a friend or family member has a birthday, write a free verse poem about that person saying what you like about him or her.

Check your progress:

Listening/Speaking: Did you write down key words as you listened to your classmates read their poems?

Reading: Did you skim through magazines to find pictures you could use for your collage?

Writing: Did you compare things using similes?

Viewing: Did you use key words to help you match the picture collages with the poems?

Use with student text page 116.

Think, Pair, Share

1. **THINK** about a woman's role in a marriage. What do you think a man's role in a marriage is? Make some notes below.

_____

_____

_____

_____

_____

2. **PAIR** with another student and tell that student what you think the roles of women and men are in marriage. Listen carefully and take notes while your partner tells you about his or her ideas.

_____

_____

_____

_____

_____

3. With your partner, join another pair of students.

4. **SHARE** with the others in the group what your partner told you about the roles of women and men in marriage. Listen as the others tell you what they heard.

5. **WRITE** a group summary of ideas about the roles of women and men in marriage.

_____

_____

_____

_____

_____

UNIT 3: LOVE

Listening/Speaking/critically.   Encourage students to actively listen and take notes as students share their ideas.

Writing/inquiry/research. Summarize.   Have students prepare a group summary.

Use with student text page 122.

"Karate" Story Map

1. After you read "Karate," analyze the story by filling in the story map below.

2. Compare your story map with another student's story map. Share your ideas with your partner. Make additions to your story map if your partner has ideas you do not have. Contribute to the class story map.

Title: _____	Author:_____
STORY ELEMENTS	
Characters:	
Setting:	
Initial event:	
Reaction:	
Goal-setting:	
Attempt to reach goal:	
Outcomes:	
Resolution:	

UNIT 3: LOVE

Writing process: pre-writing strategy. Have students use the **graphic organizer** of a story map to brainstorm before they write.

Use with student text page 123.

ACTIVITY 46 MASTER

Writing a Family Story or Incident

1. Think about an interesting incident in your life or a family story that you have heard.

2. Write a lead for your story, paying close attention to how you will set the tone and get the reader's attention. For example, "You just celebrated Martin Luther King Day and the Super Bowl. Why stop now? Get ready for more fun as the Year of the Dragon brings in the Chinese New Year."

_____

_____

_____

_____

_____

_____

_____

_____

3. Write a concluding sentence that reveals the resolution of the story and leaves a strong final impression with the reader.

_____

_____

_____

_____

_____

4. Use the Editing Checklist (Activity Master 97) on page 124 to edit your work.

5. Ask another student to read your story or incident and to offer suggestions, ideas, and comments. Rewrite your story and publish it in a class book or newspaper.

UNIT 3: LOVE

Writing process: develop a draft, revise, edit, and publish. Encourage students to develop a draft and work collaboratively toward publishing their work in a class book or newspaper.

Use with student text pages 117–121.

All Sorts of Sports: A Sports Brochure for the Community

Words to Know

sports	brochure	advertise	attract	
sport	slogan	equipment	training	practice

Project Goal: Most **sports** require **training** and **practice**, just like the sport in the story "Karate." You will choose a **sport** and find out where you can practice it in your community. Then, you will create a **brochure** to **advertise** that sport. Your goal is to **attract** more people to play that sport.

1. Choose a sport. Write a short description of the sport. Tell how and when people usually play it.

2. Next find out where people play this sport. Get information from your school or community center. Write a few lines about where to play this sport. Can you take lessons? When can you play or practice? How much does it cost? What **equipment** do you need? Is it only for certain ages?

3. Talk to people who play this sport. Ask them why they like this sport. Write down the exact words they say. Use these sentences as quotations in your brochure.
   Speaking tip: If you don't understand something, ask people to repeat or explain what they said.

4. Write a **slogan** for the sport. A slogan is a short, persuasive sentence that is easy to remember. If you are advertising swimming, you might write a slogan like, "Get wet!" Look for slogans in newspapers or sports magazines to get ideas.
   Writing tip: Think about using rhyme, alliteration, assonance, or idioms in your slogan.

5. Design your brochure. Write your slogan in large letters across the top. Put the text on the page in a way that is easy to read. Add the quotations you wrote down. Draw pictures, use photos, or get graphics from the computer if you can. Persuade your readers to try your sport!

Check your progress:

Listening/Speaking: Did you ask for repetition or explanation when you needed it?

Writing: Did you use rhyme, alliteration, assonance, or idioms in your slogan?

Viewing: Did you look for slogans in newspapers or magazines? Does your brochure design make your message easy to understand?

Learn more sports words with The Newbury House Dictionary CD-ROM, Unit 15.

UNIT 3: LOVE

THERE IS NO WORD FOR GOODBYE

ACTIVITY 47 MASTER

How Do You Say Goodbye to Your Loved Ones?

With two classmates, think of as many ways as you can to say "goodbye." These words can be in English or other languages you know.

- List the word.
- List the language of the word.
- List the English meaning of the word.

Way of saying goodbye	Language	English meaning

UNIT 3: LOVE

Writing/evaluation. Have students use a **dictionary** or **thesaurus** to determine meanings for the word "goodbye."

Use with student text page 128.

Marking a Poem

1. Find pens or pencils in three different colors.
2. Read the poem once. In the first color, highlight any words that confuse or surprise you. After reading the entire poem, check the meaning of new words in your dictionary or with a classmate.
3. Read the poem a second time. In a second color, highlight words that show a shift or change of ideas in the poem.
4. Read the poem two more times with a partner. As your partner reads the poem aloud to you, highlight the words he or she stresses. Then reverse roles for another reading.
5. Compare your highlighted poem with your partner's. Discuss any differences and similarities. Share what you have learned with the class.

There Is No Word for Goodbye

by Mary TallMountain

Sokoya, I said, looking through
    the net of wrinkles into
    wise black pools
    of her eyes.

What do you say in Athabaskan
    when you leave each other?
    What is the word
    for goodbye?

A shade of feeling rippled
    the wind-tanned skin.
    Ah, nothing, she said,
    watching the river flash.

She looked at me close.
    We just say, Tlaa. That means,
    See you.
    We never leave each other.
    When does your mouth
    say goodbye to your heart?

She touched me light
    as a bluebell.
    You forget when you leave us;
    you're so small then.
    We don't use that word.

We always think you're coming back,
    but if you don't,
    we'll see you some place else.
    You understand.
    There is no word for goodbye.

Listening/Speaking/presentations. Have students read out loud using **pitch, tone,** and **stress** as they speak.

Reading/comprehension. Students are encouraged to read using a variety of strategies such as highlighting words and reversing roles and highlighting stress to help comprehend the poem.

Use with student text page 129.

Imagery

1. In the poem "There is No Word for Goodbye," the poet uses many images from nature to share the feelings and values of the Athabaskan people. For example, she describes the old woman's eyes as "wise black pools" surrounded by a "net of wrinkles."

2. How do you think the poet feels about the old woman? Why?

_____

_____

_____

_____

_____

3. Can you find other examples of imagery from nature in the poem?

_____

_____

_____

_____

_____

4. Can you find examples of similes or metaphors in the poem? (Check Appendix B of your student text for definitions and examples of similes and metaphors.)

_____

_____

_____

_____

_____

5. What do these images tell you about the Athabaskan culture?

_____

_____

_____

_____

_____

UNIT 3: LOVE

Listening/Speaking/evaluation.   Encourage students to analyze the poem for literary elements: similes, metaphors, and imagery.
Writing/inquiry/research.   Have students write the answers to the questions above as a **study tool** to clarify and remember literary elements.

Use with student text page 129.

Descriptive Writing

1. Visit a beautiful outdoor park or garden. Fill in the chart below. Describe what you see, hear, feel, smell, or taste. Use as many descriptive words as you can.

Your Senses	Descriptions of what you see, hear, feel, smell, and taste
See	
Hear	
Feel	
Smell	
Taste	

2. Using the descriptions in the chart above, write about the place you visited. Try to use some similes and metaphors in your description.

_____

_____

_____

_____

_____

_____

_____

_____

3. Use the Editing Checklist (Activity Master 97) to edit your work.

Writing purpose: personal. Have students do **descriptive writing** using the **pre-writing** chart above as a guideline.

Use with student text pages 125–127.

Hello and Goodbye: A Guide for Newcomers

Words to Know

greet   formal   expressions   informal   gestures   wave   guidebook

Project Goal: In the Athabaskan language, there is no word for goodbye. In English, however, there are many ways to say "goodbye" and also to say "hello" (**greet** people). You are going to make a **guidebook** to help new students of English learn which **expressions** and **gestures** are appropriate in which situations.

1. In your school community, listen to people greeting and saying "goodbye" to each other. Write down the expressions you hear (for example, "Hi") and gestures you see (for example, a **wave**). Which expressions are **formal**? Which are **informal**?
    Listening tip: Listen for differences in the expressions teenagers use with other teenagers, students use with teachers, and teachers use with other teachers.

2. Working in a small group, organize the expressions and gestures you saw onto two charts, one for greeting and one for saying "goodbye." You can also add other expressions and gestures you know. Look in a thesaurus for more expressions.
    Reading tip: A thesaurus is a book of synonyms.

Ways to greet people

Expression or gesture	Who uses it	Situation
What's happening?	students with other students	at school with friends

3. Share your chart with some native speakers of English. Ask them if the information is accurate. Ask them if they can think of other expressions and gestures to add.

4. Make a "Hello and Goodbye" guidebook for students learning English. Here are some ideas you can use. Include pictures from magazines and newspapers. Draw comic strips or make games. (crossword puzzles, word finds). You can also use your own ideas.

Extend: Make a video of people greeting each other and saying "goodbye" in a variety of ways.

Check your progress:

Listening/Speaking: Did you listen for different expressions people use?

Reading: Did you check a thesaurus for synonyms?

Writing: Do you know which expressions are formal or informal?

UNIT 3: LOVE

Use with student text page 130.

What Is Love?

1. Work in a group of about four students to fill in the chart below. Fill in one thing that "love is" to you. Pass the chart to another student, and he or she will fill in something that "love is" or "love is not" to him or her. Continue to pass the chart around until it is complete or until no one has anything else to add.

2. When your chart is complete, share it with the class and make a class chart on love.

LOVE IS, LOVE IS NOT	
Love is	**Love is not**

Second language/reading. Have students use the two-column **graphic organizer** to prepare for reading the selection on love.

Use with student text page 134.

Two-Column Chart (T-List)

1. Write some metaphors about what love is and is not. Use this T-List to organize your ideas.
2. Illustrate your metaphors with paintings or drawings.

LOVE IS, LOVE IS NOT	
Love is	**Love is not**

Writing process.   Have students use the **pre-writing strategy** of a graphic organizer (T-List) to organize their ideas.

UNIT 3: LOVE

Use with student text page 135.

Responding to Poetry

1. Meet with a writing-response group of four students. Take turns reading your love metaphor poems aloud.

2. After each person reads, offer some encouragement and feedback on the poem. Use the poetry response form below to remember ideas for your responses.

3. Revise your love metaphor poem based on the ideas your classmates give you, and prepare the poem for publication.

Different poems mean different things to different people at different times, but that isn't something that you need to think about when you read a poem. In fact, worrying about finding the "right" meaning can get in the way of your liking and understanding poetry. Just as you don't have to understand everything about your friends in order to enjoy them and to learn things from them, so you don't have to understand everything about a poem to like it and get something from it. Whatever you get from a poem is fine. Maybe you'll like a kind of strangeness, for instance, or a poem's sound, its words, its subject, the way it goes from one line to the next, or the mood it puts you in. Maybe you'll like the way it seems to get something just right; or what it makes you remember, and think about, and feel; or the way it makes you suddenly understand something more clearly. Poetry can be satisfying and exciting while it remains a little mysterious.

—Kate Farrell

Poetry Response Form	
What did you like about this poem?	
What did you like about the words and they way they sound?	
What did you like about the subject?	
What did you like about the poem's mysteriousness?	
What did you like about the way the words appear on the page?	
What did you like about the mood the poem puts you in?	
What did you like about what it makes you remember?	
What did you like about what it makes you think about or feel?	

Writing/evaluation. Have students work collaboratively using this **Poetry Response Form** to revise and offer suggestions about their classmates' writing.

Use with student text pages 131–133.

Writing: a Biography

Words to Know

biography   influence   background   chronological order

Project Goal: Carl Sandburg was a famous writer of poetry and biographies. Who is your favorite author in *Voices in Literature*? What do you know about him or her? You will choose an author and write a **biography**. You will research his or her **background** and write how you think it **influenced** his or her writing.

1. Scan the reading selections in the student text and select one author to write about. Make a list of questions about the author you want answered, for example, what was the author's childhood like? Where did the author live? Was English his or her first language? What other kind of books or poetry has he or she written? This will help to direct your research.
    > **Reading tip:** Use a chart like the one in Activity Master 22 (Culture Map) on page 28 to organize your research.

2. Go to the library and look in encyclopedias, books, and on the Internet. Skim and scan for the answers to the questions you wrote on the Culture Map. You can also talk to other people in your school and community and find out what they may know about the author. Take notes.

3. Using your notes, write a draft of your biography. Share your work with a partner. Use Activity Masters 96 and 97 on pages 123–124 to revise your work and create a final draft. Use a word processing program if you have a computer.
    > **Writing tip:** Include only the most important events in the author's life. Write the events in **chronological order** (from the beginning of the author's life to the end or the present).

4. Find a photo of the author or a painting or illustration that you feel represents his or her life and work. Look at the illustration that relates to his or her work in *Voices in Literature* if you need ideas. Put this illustration on the front page of your report to create a cover. Publish the collection as a class anthology of biographies.

5. Divide into small groups. Each person in the group will present a biography. Answer any questions your classmates may have. After everyone has presented, compare the authors. What are some of their similarities and differences? Why do you think they chose to become authors?

Extend: The next time you read a story you like, look up information about the author.

Check your progress:

Listening/Speaking: Did you answer the questions the class had?

Reading: Did you skim and scan for information while you did your research?

Writing: Did you use the Activity Masters to revise your rough draft?

Viewing: Did you find a photo of the author or a picture that represents his or her life?

UNIT 3: LOVE

Use with student text page 136.

Love Quickwrite

1. Think about what you would say to someone you love if you thought you might never see him or her again.

2. Write for five to ten minutes. Write everything that comes into your head about what you would say to the person you love. Write down as many ideas as you can, without worrying about your spelling, grammar, and punctuation. You can correct your work later.

_____

_____

_____

_____

_____

_____

_____

_____

_____

_____

_____

_____

_____

_____

_____

_____

3. When you finish writing, share your draft with a group of three or four classmates. Talk about what you have heard.

4. Select your group's favorite story and share it with the entire class.

Writing process: pre-writing strategy. Students do a **quickwrite** and share their draft with the group.

UNIT 3: LOVE

Use with student text page 142.

Powerful Words

1. Sullivan Ballou wrote powerfully about two things he loved, country and family. Look for ideas and phrases that he used to express his love for his country and his love for his family.

2. Write and draw these ideas on the chart below.

SULLIVAN BALLOU'S TWO LOVES	
Country	**Family**

UNIT 3: LOVE

Reading/word identification/vocabulary development. Students rely on context to determine the meaning and connection between ideas and phrases that express love of country and family.

Writing process: pre-writing strategy. Have students use the graphic organizer (two columns) to collect ideas for writing.

Use with student text page 143.

Conflict in Sullivan Ballou's Letter

Sullivan Ballou wrote powerfully about conflict between his duty to his country and his duty to his family. Look for ideas and phrases that express his duty to his country and his duty to his family. Write and/or draw these examples of conflict on the chart below.

CONFLICT IN SULLIVAN BALLOU'S LETTER	
Duty to Country	**Duty to Family**

UNIT 3: LOVE

Reading/word identification/vocabulary development.   Students rely on context to determine the meaning and connection between ideas and phrases that express conflict between love of country and family.

Writing process: pre-writing strategy.   Have students use the graphic organizer to list ideas for writing.

THE SULLIVAN BALLOU LOVE LETTER

Use with student text page 144.

Contrast in Sullivan Ballou's Letter

1. Sullivan Ballou describes objects or ideas by comparing them with something quite different. For example, Ballou contrasts the strong wind that takes men to war with the soft breeze of his own breath on his wife's cheek. Look for examples of contrast in the letter.

2. Write and/or draw the examples of contrast on the chart below.

CONTRAST IN SULLIVAN BALLOU'S LETTER	
A strong wind that takes men to war.	*A soft breeze of his own breath on his wife's cheek.*

UNIT 3: LOVE

Copyright © 2001 Heinle & Heinle

Writing process: pre-writing strategy. Students use this graphic organizer (two columns) to list contrasts as they analyze literature and prepare to write.

Use with student text pages 144–145.

Writing a Personal Letter

1. Reread the quickwrite you wrote before you read "The Sullivan Ballou Love Letter." Use some of the ideas you wrote there to write a personal letter to someone you love.
2. Use a new paragraph for each new idea in your letter.
3. For the closing of the letter, use a phrase such as *Love*, *Fondly*, or *Truly yours*.
4. Use the format below to write your letter.

_____
(Address)

_____
(City, State, Zip code)

_____
(Date)

Dear _____,
(Salutation—"Dear [name of person you're writing to]")

_____

_____

_____

_____

_____

_____

_____

_____

_____

_____

_____,
(Closing—"Love," "Fondly," or "Truly yours")

_____
(Signature of writer)

UNIT 3: LOVE

Body (Use a paragraph for each main idea.)

Copyright © 2001 Heinle & Heinle

Writing/purposes. Students write a letter as a personal **response to literature.**

ACTIVITY **59** MASTER

Writing a Historical Love Letter

Using the ideas from your quickwrite, write a historical love letter from someone who is about to be separated from a loved one by a historical event. Read about the event so that historical facts will be correct. Follow the standard format below.

_____

(Address)

_____

(City, State, Zip code)

_____

(Date)

Dear _____,

(Salutation—"Dear [name of person you're writing to]")

_____

_____

Body (Use a paragraph for each main idea.)

_____

_____

_____

_____

_____

_____

_____

_____

_____

_____

_____,

(Closing—something like "Yours truly" or "Sincerely")

_____

(Signature of writer)

Copyright © 2001 Heinle & Heinle

UNIT 3: LOVE

Writing/purposes.   Students write a historical letter as a personal **response to literature**.

Use with student text pages 137–141.

Civil War Experts: Create a Class Newspaper

Words to Know

Civil War	newspapers	timeline	headline	article	caption
battle	Underground Railroad	freedom	publish	layout	

Project Goal: Did you know there were **newspapers** more than 100 years ago, at the time that *The Sullivan Ballou Love Letter* was written? You will create several pages of a newspaper published in 1861, just after the beginning of the **Civil War**.

1. With a partner, research one of these topics and write a newspaper **article**:
    *   The Battle of Bull Run (the battle mentioned in *The Sullivan Ballou Love Letter*). Include the date, location, and outcome of the **battle**. Who won and lost?
    *   Abraham Lincoln, president during the Civil War. Include his accomplishments through 1861.
    *   The **Underground Railroad**. What was it? How did it help slaves and the cause of **freedom**?
    *   The Civil War from the beginning (1860) up to the Battle of Bull Run in 1861. Make a **timeline** of battles to help you.
    *   Another related topic of your choice.
        > **Research tip:** Look in encyclopedias, books, and on the Internet. Try to find actual newspapers written at that time. Take notes. Look up any unfamiliar words.

2. Write a draft of the newspaper article. Make it about 2-3 paragraphs long. In the first paragraph, answer the "Wh" questions: Who? What? When? Where? and Why?. Be sure to include a **headline**. Reread and edit the article using the Editing Checklist (Activity Master 97). Write a final draft. Make a copy of a photograph or map from your research and include it with your article. Write a **caption**, or brief explanation of it. Write a conclusion for your article.
    > **Writing tip**: Be sure to get the attention of your audience in your first paragraph. What will people want to find out about your topic?

3. Gather all the articles for the newspaper. If possible, use a word processing program. Create a name for your newspaper. Decide on the **layout**, or how to place the articles on the page.
    > **Viewing tip:** Look at your local newspaper for ideas on how to layout articles.

4. "**Publish**" the newspaper and read all the articles. Discuss how you did your research. Listen for tips from others. Share your newspaper with your History or Social Studies class.

Extend: Create a newspaper on another topic. Publish articles in your school newspaper.

Check your progress:

Listening/Speaking: Did you listen carefully to how others did research?

Reading: Did you take notes? Did you look up unfamiliar words?

Writing: Did you use encyclopedias, the Internet, or other sources of information?

Viewing: Did you look at local newspapers to see how they are laid out? Did this help you?

UNIT 3: LOVE

Use with student text page 146.

Ranking Ladder

1. Think about qualities and characteristics that you think a person should look for in a boyfriend or a girlfriend. Write down all the ideas you can think of.

_____

_____

_____

_____

2. Now rank all the above ideas on the ranking ladder. Put the most important ideas at the top and the least important ideas at the bottom.

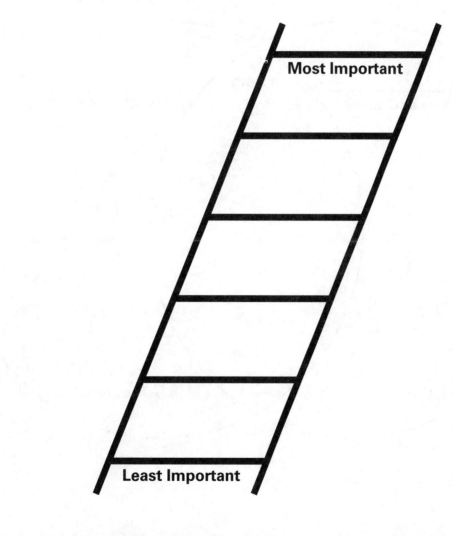

Most Important

Least Important

Copyright © 2001 Heinle & Heinle

UNIT 3: LOVE

Writing process: pre-writing strategy.   Have students use the graphic organizer to rank their ideas.

Use with student text pages 164–165.

Comparing and Contrasting Literature

1. Work with a small group to compare and contrast the "Balcony Scene from *West Side Story*" and the "Balcony Scene from *Romeo and Juliet*" on a Venn diagram.

2. Choose an element from the two plays to compare and contrast—for example, plot, conflict, leads, conclusions, or metaphors.

3. Fill in the larger circles with information from each play.

4. Look for ways the two are alike, and fill in the middle section of the Venn diagram.

5. Share your Venn diagram with your class.

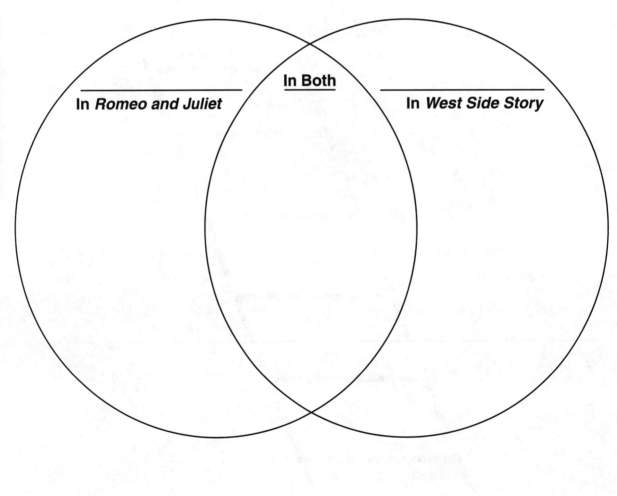

In Both

In *Romeo and Juliet*

In *West Side Story*

Writing process: pre-writing strategy. Students use this **graphic organizer** (Venn diagram) to compare and contrast the elements of a story, i.e. plot, conflict, leads, conclusions, or metaphors.

Use with student text page 165.

Comparing Characters

1. Select two characters from the balcony scenes to compare and contrast. Write the names of these characters on the lines at the tops of the circles.

2. Reread the two balcony scenes to find descriptions or actions of the characters. Fill in the sides of the circles with the descriptions and actions unique to each character. Fill in the middle of the two circles with elements that are common to both characters. In parentheses, write the page and line numbers by each description or action you find—for example:

   Tony: "I'm not afraid." (*page 153, line 13*)

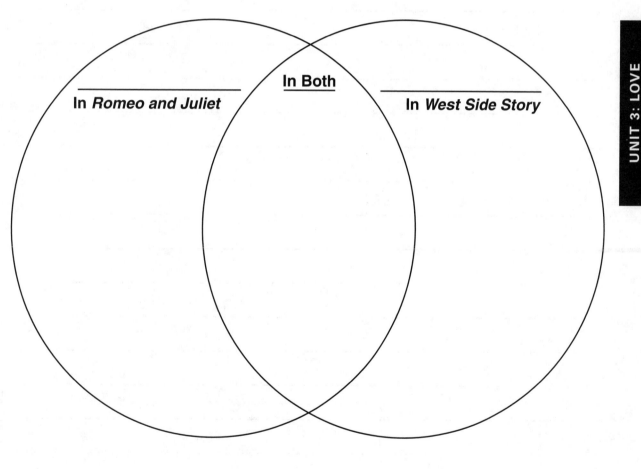

In *Romeo and Juliet*

In Both

In *West Side Story*

UNIT 3: LOVE

Listening/Speaking/evaluation: Character Development.   Students work collaboratively, comparing and contrasting how the authors treat character development in two plays about love.

Writing process: pre-writing strategy.   Students use the **graphic organizer** (Venn diagram) to compare characters.

Writing about Two Characters

Look at the Venn diagram you made comparing two characters on Activity Master 62. Use the ideas you wrote there to write a short essay comparing and contrasting the two characters. Use quotations from the two balcony scenes to support your ideas. Here are a few reminders:

- Always put the speaker's words in quotation marks.

- Use a slash (/) to show where a new line starts—for example, "Arise, fair sun, and kill the envious moon/Who is already sick and pale with grief."

_____

_____

_____

_____

_____

_____

_____

_____

_____

_____

_____

_____

_____

_____

_____

_____

UNIT 3: LOVE

Writing/purpose. Have students write a **five-paragraph persuasive** or **reflective essay** comparing the two characters. Have them use the three parts of an essay: introduction, body (three points with reasons and elaboration after each), and a conclusion and the **Editing Checklist** on Activity Master 97 to check **punctuation, spelling,** and **organization**.

Use with student text pages 147–155 and 157–163.

Act It Out: A Reader's Theater Project

Words to Know

scene   character   play   gestures   conflict

Project Goal: *Romeo and Juliet* is a powerful love story. Actors express the emotion of words with voice and movement. In this project, you will create a Reader's Theater **play**. Remember to use expression and emotion when you speak your part.

1. Listen to the selections from *West Side Story* and *Romeo and Juliet* on the *Voices in Literature* audiocassette. If there is a video of *West Side Story*, watch the **scene** in which Tony and Maria sing "Tonight." How do the actors in both selections show their feelings in their voices? In their **gestures** (if you have a video)? Write three things that you notice about their voices or gestures.

2. Imagine that *West Side Story* and *Romeo and Juliet* were written this year. Imagine that Tony and Maria or Romeo and Juliet are living now. How old do you think they are? What do you think they might wear? Where are their families from? Where do they live? Why are their families in **conflict**? Discuss in small groups.

3. Working alone, imagine you are Tony or Maria living today. Write a letter to your parents about your girlfriend (Maria or Juliet) or your boyfriend (Tony or Romeo). Explain how you feel about the conflict. Explain how you feel about your girlfriend or boyfriend. Persuade your parents to accept your situation.

     Writing tip: Think of the **character's** point of view. Use a respectful voice for the letter. Remember you are writing to your parents. Use Activity Master 58 on page 74.

4. Choose either the scene from *West Side Story* or *Romeo and Juliet*. Write some or all of the scene in your own words. Think about how teenagers really talk today. Practice the scene with a partner or partners before you perform your scene for the class. Compare the original text and video version with your Reader's Theater version.

Check your progress:

Listening/Speaking: What similarities and differences did you find when you compared your version to the original text?

Writing: Did you write the letter from the point of view of the character? Did you use respectful language?

Viewing: Did you compare your version to the original text or the video?

UNIT 3: LOVE

Write a Compare/Contrast Essay

Words to Use

I prefer	alike	but	in my opinion	on the other hand
even though	same	different	however	

Goal: You are going to write an essay that compares and contrasts the book and the movie of *Romeo and Juliet* or *West Side Story*. You will use the prompt, or writing assignment, below. Follow each step carefully.

1. Read the prompt, or writing assignment. What will you be writing about? Who is your audience? Focus on the purpose of your writing: to compare and contrast reading a book with watching a movie.

Prompt: Compare and contrast reading the book and watching the movie of *Romeo and Juliet* or *West Side Story*. How is the experience of reading literature the same or different from watching the movie? Which do you prefer?

2. Make a chart to compare reading a book and watching a movie. Add your own ideas.

READING	WATCHING
easy to stop and look up a word	not so easy to stop and ask for a word
sometimes I get lost without pictures	pictures help me understand

3. Next, organize your essay. Use a Venn diagram. In each large circle, list ways that reading and listening are different. Where the circles overlap, list ways they are alike.

4. Write a draft of five paragraphs. (Don't forget to indent!) Write five sentences for paragraphs 2, 3, and 4. Use words from Words to Use above.

   • Paragraph 1: Start your essay with a topic sentence. Get your reader's attention. Briefly tell about the two ways of enjoying literature. Tell which you prefer.
   • Paragraph 2: State ways that reading the book and watching the movie are alike.
   • Paragraph 3: State ways that they are different.
   • Paragraph 4: State reasons why you prefer either reading the book or watching the movie.
   • Paragraph 5: Summarize the ways reading and viewing are alike or different. Use your last sentence to tell which you prefer and why.

Work with a partner and give each other feedback. Use Activity Master 96 on page 123.

5. Write your final draft. Read and compare your preference with others in the class.

UNIT 3: LOVE

Copyright © 2001 Heinle & Heinle

Use with student text page 170.

Remembering

1. What do you do to remember things you need to remember? One person might change her watch to the opposite wrist while another person might write a note. Draw a picture and write about the ways you remember things.

```
┌─────────────────────────────────────┐
│                                       │
│                                       │
│                                       │
│                                       │
│                                       │
│                                       │
└─────────────────────────────────────┘
```

_____

_____

_____

_____

_____

_____

_____

2. Work with a group of students and compare your ideas about the ways you remember things. Share your group's ideas with the whole class.

UNIT 4: ADVICE

Writing purpose: personal. Encourage students to write a paragraph about their personal memory techniques.

Listening/Speaking: purposes. Students make relevant contributions to a discussion by comparing ways they remember things.

Use with student text page 174.

Ranking Ladder for Things to Remember

1. Work with a partner and list the things the poet Joy Harjo wants you to remember in the poem "Remember." Look at the list and group similar things into categories. For example, the sun, moon, and stars might be grouped under the category "heavenly bodies." Use the chart below.

Heavenly Bodies					
sun moon stars					

2. Take the category headings and list them on the ranking ladder in the order you feel is the most important to remember. Write the most important things to remember at the top of the ladder and the least important things on the bottom of the ladder.

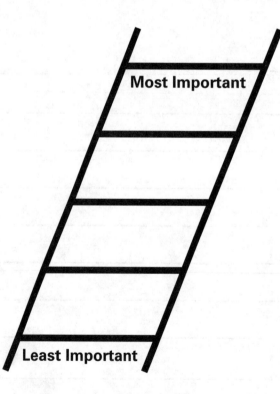

3. Compare your ladder with other ladders made by your team. Are they the same? Are they different? Explain to your team why you placed each category on the ladder where you did.

Reading/inquiry/research: graphic feature. Students refer to a poem about things to remember and make categories.
Writing process: pre-writing strategy. Students use the graphic organizer of a Ranking Ladder to rank categories.
Listening/Speaking: purposes. Students discuss, compare, contrast, and explain their ladders.

Use with student text page 175.

Repetition

1. What words are repeated in the poem "Remember"?

_____

_____

_____

_____

2. What sentence patterns are repeated?

_____

_____

_____

_____

3. What words are repeated in combination with different words?

_____

_____

_____

_____

4. What is the effect of this repetition?

_____

_____

_____

_____

UNIT 4: ADVICE

Reading/comprehension.   Students study a literary device, repetition, to better understand its use in a poem.

Writing/inquiry/research.   Students use this writing activity to serve as a study tool to clarify what is meant by repetition.

Listening/Speaking: purposes.   Encourage students to work in pairs and discuss their answers.

An Advice Poem

1. Write a poem that offers advice to someone else. Use one of the following words or phrases to begin each line of your poem. You can use these words and phrases in any order.

- *Remember*
- *Forget*
- *Do*
- *Do not*
- *Seek*
- *Watch out for*

2. Use the Editing Checklist (Activity Master 97) to edit your work.

_____

_____

_____

_____

_____

_____

_____

_____

_____

_____

_____

_____

_____

_____

UNIT 4: ADVICE

Copyright © 2001 Heinle & Heinle

Writing purpose: Poetry. Students write a poem that offers advice to someone else, using special words such as: *Remember, Forget, Do, Do not, Seek, Watch out for.*

Writing/grammar/usage/conventions/spelling. Students edit their work with the Editing Checklist.

Use with student text pages 171–173.

Art to Remember: A Fine Art Book

Words to Know

| vivid | images | reread | fine art | illustrate |

Project Goal: In the poem "Remember," Joy Harjo uses **vivid** language. Her poem creates pictures in your mind. In this project, you will use these mental pictures, or **images**, to create a **fine art** book to accompany the poem. You will then present and display the book to your classmates.

1. **Reread** the poem "Remember" on pages 171–173 of your student text. Make a list, in note form, of the things the author tells you to remember.
   Reading tip: To take good notes, you do not need to write every word of the idea, just enough words to help you remember the idea (for example: *sky, sun's birth, sundown*).

2. Work in a small group. Choose some images from the poem that you would like to **illustrate**. Brainstorm creative ways to illustrate them. For example, the poet refers to the wind as "her," so you could draw the wind as a woman.
   Viewing tip: For ideas, look at the art that illustrates the poem on page 172 of your student text. Why do you think it was chosen?

3. Assign each person in your group to illustrate several images. Use pencils, colored pencils, magic markers, paint, or other materials to illustrate your pictures. Then label each picture. For example, you could paint a sunrise and label it "the strongest point of time."

4. Combine your labeled illustrations and those of your classmates into a book called "Remember."

5. Practice the presentation you will give to another group. Divide up the poem and decide which person in your group will read each part. Practice reading your part of the poem to your group. Give each other suggestions for improving the presentation.
   Speaking tip: Practice pronouncing words clearly and with expression.

6. Present your poem to another group or to the class. Hold up the pictures as you speak.

Extend: Write and illustrate a "Remember" poem for your imaginary great-grandchildren. Tell them things you want them to remember about their backgrounds.

Check your progress:

Listening/Speaking: Did you pronounce your words clearly during your presentation?
Writing: Did you take notes by writing down just the important words?
Viewing: Did you look at the art in your student text for ideas?

UNIT 4: ADVICE

Use with student text page 176.

Rules Brainstorm

1. Advice comes in many forms. Sometimes rules are considered advice since they tell us what we can and cannot do. List some of the rules or "dos and don'ts" that you hear at home or school.

_____

_____

_____

_____

_____

_____

_____

_____

_____

_____

2. Share your list of rules with a small group of students. Listen to the rules other students wrote. Add rules you don't have to your list above.

3. Pick one rule that is the same for all the students in your group. Why do you think this rule is one that everyone must follow?

_____

_____

_____

_____

Writing process: pre-writing strategy. Have students brainstorm a list of rules as a draft for writing.

Listening/Speaking: purposes. Have students work in small groups to share their lists of rules.

UNIT 4: ADVICE

Use with student text page 180.

Ironic or Metaphorical Advice

1. Karla Kuskin's "Rules" can be read as ironic; that is, the poem is making fun of rules. "Rules" can also be read as metaphorical. For example, "Do not jump on ancient uncles" may mean "pay attention to the wisdom of the past." List rules from the poem on the left side of the chart below. Then write what you think they mean in the right-hand column.

Rule	Meaning

2. Compare the meanings you wrote with the meanings other students wrote. Revise what you wrote. Compile a class chart of all the possible meanings for a rule.

UNIT 4: ADVICE

Writing process: pre-writing strategy. Have students use the graphic organizer above to write a draft about the meaning of rules in ironic or metaphorical ways.

Listening/Speaking. Have partners take turns rereading with expression the poem "Rules."

Use with student text page 180.

Writing Rules

1. Before you read the poem "Rules," you wrote a list of rules. Copy three of the rules you wrote. Rewrite these rules into an ironic or metaphorical rule like one of Kuskin's. Here are some hints for rewriting your rules:

   • Write the opposite.
   • Put the rule in an unusual setting.
   • Make the rule about animals.

Your Rule	Your Rewritten Rule

2. Read your rewritten rules out loud to a group of classmates. Take notes on revisions you might use to make them better.

_____

_____

_____

3. Revise your rules, and when you think they are ready, copy them on the next page. Illustrate and publish your page as part of a class book or post it on the bulletin board as part of a class display.

_____

_____

_____

_____

UNIT 4: ADVICE

Reading/comprehension (ESL).   Students can use a **graphic organizer** as a pre-reading activity to prepare for reading a poem.
Writing process: pre-writing strategy.   Have students use the graphic organizer as a pre-writing activity for rewriting, revising, and publishing their rules as part of a class book or display.

Use with student text page 180.

1. Rewrite and illustrate your group's revised rules on this page.

2. Copy the page. Publish each group's rules by displaying them or putting them together in a class book of rules.

𝕽𝖚𝖑𝖊𝖘

UNIT 4: ADVICE

Writing process: pre-writing strategy.   Have students use the graphic organizer on page 90 as a pre-writing activity and then rewrite, revise, and publish their rules as part of a class book or display.

Use with student text page 181.

Poetic Rhythm

How to Scan a Poem:

Scanning is a way to record the rhythm of a poem. To "scan" a poem, we use symbols to mark syllables as accented (stressed) or unaccented (unstressed). We tend to pronounce the accented syllables more loudly. Use the following steps to scan a poem:

1. Work with a small group.

2. Copy the poem "Rules" onto your own paper. Each person should have a copy.

3. Listen as someone reads the poem one line at a time.

4. Mark the stressed syllables with " ◢ ".

5. Mark unstressed syllables with " ◡ ". The first line of this poem would look like this:

      ◢   ◡   ◢   ◡   ◢   ◡   ◢   ◡

   Do not jump on an- cient un- cles.

6. Count how many syllables are in each line. How many syllables are accented?

Challenge:

Below are four types of poetic rhythm or "feet" and an example of each. Look for other examples in poems you have read. What kind of "feet" does the poem "Rules" have?

◡ ◢	**iamb:**	an unstressed syllable followed by a stressed syllable
		Example: giraffe (◡ ◢)
◢ ◡	**trochee:**	a stressed syllable followed by an unstressed syllable
		Example: monkey (◢ ◡)
◡ ◡ ◢	**anapest:**	two unstressed syllables followed by a stressed syllable
		Example: little snake (◡◡ ◢)
◢ ◡ ◡	**dactyl:**	a stressed syllable followed by two unstressed syllables
		Example: elephant (◢◡ ◡)

UNIT 4: ADVICE

Listening/Speaking/evaluation. Students listen to and analyze the language of poetry for accented (stressed) and unaccented (unstressed) syllables.

Use with student text page 181.

Humorous Advice

1. Collect and read advice columns from the newspaper. What kinds of problems do people write about? Think of an "advice column" question and write it below.

_____

_____

_____

2. Exchange questions with another student in the class. Write an "advice column" to answer your classmate's question.

_____

_____

_____

_____

_____

_____

_____

_____

_____

_____

_____

_____

_____

_____

_____

3. Exchange your paper with another student and edit his or her paper using the Editing Checklist (Activity Master 97).

UNIT 4: ADVICE

Reading/variety of sources: newspapers. Have students collect and read advice columns from newspapers or electronic texts.

Writing purposes. Students write an "advice column."

Writing/evaluation. Students use the Editing Checklist to check spelling, punctuation, grammar, and organization.

Use with student text pages 177–179.

Humorous Rules: A Poster of Laughs

Words to Know

humor   humorous   negative   laugh   make fun of   poster

Project Goal: Karla Kuskin **makes fun of** advice in her poem "Rules." Sometimes advice is easier to accept if it makes you **laugh**. You have a chance to give advice or "rules" in a **humorous** way. You will make a **poster** of the advice to show in class.

1. In small groups or with a partner, make a list of advice for one of the following:
    * doing well in school
    * getting a job after school
    * getting to school on time
    * choose your own idea

2. Write the same advice, but in **negative** form. Express the negative advice in a humorous way. Use a chart like the one below:

Advice for doing well in school

Advice	Negative form of advice
Concentrate when you study.	Don't study like a frog, hopping away from your books.
Ask questions in class.	Don't sit silently in class like a sleeping cat. Open your mouth and ask questions.
Study with friends.	Don't study alone. Misery loves company.

3. Create a poster with your humorous advice. Draw pictures or cut out pictures from a magazine to illustrate your advice. Write the humorous advice in large letters so that people can read the poster from far away. Share your poster with the class.

4. Look at ads or billboards, listen to the radio, or watch TV commercials that persuade people to do or not do something. (For example, look at ads against smoking!) What words do you read or hear? What images do you see? Is humor used in the message? Do the ads persuade you? Share your ideas with the class.

Extend: The next time you give advice, use **humor** to make a point or get attention.

Check your progress:

Listening/Speaking: Did you listen to ads and analyze how they persuade people?
Reading: Did you create your poster based on the information in your chart?
Writing: Did you write negative sentences beginning with "Don't"?
Viewing: Did you view posters or ads and analyze how they persuade people?

Use with student text page 182.

Interviews:
What Is a True Friend?

1. Interview five people. Ask them, "What is a true friend?" Take notes on the chart below.

Name	What is a true friend?

2. Fill in the cluster map below with the characteristics you found in the interviews. List each characteristic only once. Add more circles if you have more characteristics. Add details to the characteristics. For example, if the characteristic is "happy," you might add "tells jokes, smiles, is easygoing."

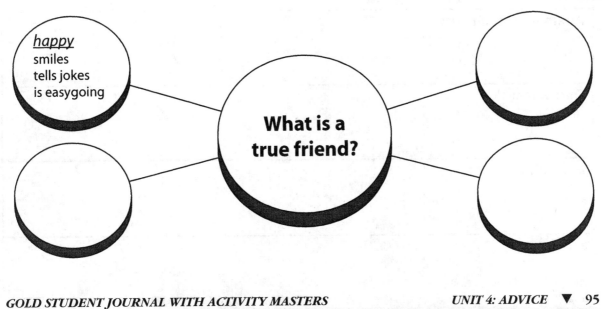

UNIT 4: ADVICE

Listening/Speaking purposes. Students interview five people, asking them, "What is a true friend?" They actively listen to the responses to the questions.

Writing process: pre-writing strategy. Students complete a cluster map about characteristics of true friends.

Use with student text page 186.

"A Mother's Advice" Story Map

Use the story map below to outline the main story elements in "A Mother's Advice."

Title: _____ Author:_____	
STORY ELEMENTS	
Characters:	
Setting:	
Initial event:	
Reaction:	
Goal-setting:	
Attempt to reach goal:	
Outcomes:	
Resolution:	

Writing process: pre-writing strategy. Have students use the graphic organizer (Story Map) to outline the main events in the reading selection, "A Mother's Advice."

UNIT 4: ADVICE

A MOTHER'S ADVICE

Use with student text page 187.

The Number Three *in Folktales*

Think of folktales that you know in which something comes in *threes*. Fill in the chart below with the name of the folktale, characters or events that come in *threes*, and contrasts or extremes shown.

Folktale	Characters or Events that Come in *Threes*	Contrasts or Extremes Shown
Goldilocks and the Three Bears	*bears, bowls of porridge, chairs, beds*	*big, bigger, biggest*

Copyright © 2001 Heinle & Heinle

UNIT 4: ADVICE

GOLD STUDENT JOURNAL WITH ACTIVITY MASTERS   *UNIT 4: ADVICE* ▼ 97

Listening/Speaking. Have partners take turns reading or telling folktales, and listening for and naming the elements of this genre.

Use with student text pages 187–188.

Static and Dynamic Characters

Look back over stories in your book and think about the characters. Are they static or dynamic? Think about the character's personality and actions at the beginning of the story and then at the end of the story. If they changed, the character is dynamic. If they did not change, the character is static. Fill in the chart below.

Character	Description and actions at the beginning of the story	Description and actions at the end of the story	Dynamic (changed) or Static (stayed the same)
Lorena, in "The Raiders Jacket"	Lorena gets excited when Eddie lends her his jacket.	Lorena turns away from romance and buys practical gifts for her mom.	Dynamic
Rachel, in "Eleven"			
The Wise Woman, in "The Wise Woman of Córdoba"			

UNIT 4: ADVICE

Writing process/inquiry/research. Have students use the **pre-writing strategy** of a graphic organizer (Static and Dynamic Characters chart) to write about characters in selections they have read (see page 99). Tell them to support their findings with examples on the chart above.

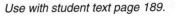

Use with student text page 189.

ACTIVITY 79 MASTER

Writing about Characterization

1. Select a favorite character from this story or other stories in *Voices in Literature*. Look at pages 187–188 in your student text about static and dynamic characters. Decide if your favorite character is static or dynamic.

2. Write an essay about this character. Start the essay with a *thesis statement*, a statement of your main idea. The thesis should state whether you think the character is static or dynamic. Next, support your thesis with details describing the character. Finally, restate your thesis in a different way.

3. Revise your essay using the Editing Checklist (Activity Master 97).

_____

_____

_____

_____

_____

_____

_____

_____

_____

_____

_____

_____

_____

_____

_____

_____

_____

UNIT 4: ADVICE

Writing purposes: persuasive. Have students write a **five-point persuasive essay** about their favorite character from a story. Have them choose either a static or dynamic character. Remind them to begin their essay with a thesis statement. Tell them to list a reason for each of the five points and to restate the thesis in a slightly different way in the conclusion.

Use with student text pages 183–185.

Giving and Getting Advice:
Write an Advice Column

Words to Know

advice	think	advice column	suggest
believe	should	audience	problem

Project Goal: In "A Mother's Advice," Selim's mother gives him some important **advice** about how to choose friends. Have you ever given advice to someone else? Well, here is your chance. You will write an **advice column** for a newspaper and then present it to the class in the form of a talk show.

1. Work in groups of three or four. As a group, list several **problems** that you might need advice about. Do you need advice about how to tell your good friend something difficult? Do you want to make more friends or need to make better use of your time? One or two of you will write a letter to "Smart Sally" asking for advice. "Smart Sally" is the writer of the advice column. One or two of you will play the role of Smart Sally and write a letter that gives advice. Include words like **believe**, **think**, **should**, and **suggest** in the advice letter.
   Reading tip: Think of your **audience**. Choose a topic that is interesting to read about. Read advice columns in the newspaper for ideas.
   Writing tip: Use Activity Master 58 (Writing a Personal Letter) on page 74 to help you.

2. Write a first and then a final draft of the letter asking Smart Sally for advice and of the letter with her response. If you have access to a computer and printer, use them to publish your advice column. Print out all the columns and display them in your classroom.
   Writing tip: Share your first drafts with your group. Ask for feedback to help you improve your letters. Did you state the problem clearly?

3. Now your group will discuss the problems you wrote about on a TV talk show! Choose one person in your group to be the host. One person will be the person seeking advice. Have the host discuss a solution to the problem with the others in your group.
   Listening/Speaking tip: Watch TV talk shows and read advice columns in newspapers. Look and listen for strong words that help convince audiences that the advice should be followed. Try to use these words in your talk show discussion to persuade others that your advice is the best.

Check your progress:

Listening/Speaking: Did you watch TV talk shows and notice strong words used in giving advice? Did you use any of them in your talk show?

Reading: Did you read advice columns in newspapers to give you ideas for writing your letters?

Writing: Did you use Activity Master 58 on page 74 to set up your letter correctly?

Viewing: Did you notice differences in the effectiveness of getting and giving advice in a newspaper column and a TV talk show?

UNIT 4: ADVICE

Use with student text page 194.

Drawing Life's Stairway

1. Draw and label a stairway, road, or path that reflects your life or the life of someone in your family. The following questions might help you:

   • Are there twists and turns in your life? What are they?

   • Are all the steps the same height? Why or why not?

   • Is part of this stairway or road in the future and part in the past? How are the parts different?

2. Write a short description of what you drew.

_____

_____

_____

_____

_____

_____

_____

UNIT 4: ADVICE

Reading/word identification/vocabulary development.   Students read and understand analogies in "Mother to Son."
Writing purposes: personal.   Have students write a short, descriptive paragraph in response to literature.

Use with student text page 195.

The Writing Process:
Using an Analogy

1. Pre-writing

Decide which analogy you will write about. Look at student text page 195 for ideas. Then think about your writing, gather ideas and information, and make plans. You might use a cluster map or a Venn diagram.

2. Drafting

Get your ideas down on paper. Try to write quickly and fluidly, and not to worry now about details like spelling and punctuation. Try a quickwrite.

3. Sharing

Share your writing with a partner or small group. When you respond to others' writing, remember:

First, offer encouragement and tell them the parts you like.

Second, ask questions to help the writer come up with more information or ideas. Was the analogy clear? What could the writer do to make it clearer?

Third, offer suggestions for improving or polishing the writing.

4. Revising

After you get ideas and suggestions from your peers and your teacher, add needed information, delete unnecessary information, clarify details, improve word choices, and organize the piece.

5. Editing

Use the Editing Checklist on page 124 to check your own work for improvements needed in spelling, usage, punctuation, arrangement of words on the page, etc. You might like to trade papers with a partner and proof each other's work.

6. Publishing

Share your work with the world! Here are some ways to publish:

- *Put it in a book in the class or school library.*
- *Read it aloud to the class.*
- *Post it on the wall in the classroom or hall.*
- *Read it to the school on a video broadcast.*
- *Make an accordion book.*
- *Send it through E-mail.*
- *Submit it to the school paper or literary magazine.*

Writing process. Encourage students to use the **pre-writing strategy** of a Venn diagram or a cluster map to list their ideas for writing a comparison. They then share, revise, and publish their writing.

UNIT 4: ADVICE

Use with student text pages 191–193.

Lessons Learned: A Reflective Essay

Words to Know

reflective essay   admire   "yes/no" questions   open-ended questions

Project Goal: In the poem "Mother to Son," Langston Hughes writes about his mother's advice. He reflects on her life. You will write a **reflective essay** about a person in your life whom you **admire**, and tell what you have learned from the person.

1. Work in a small group. Talk about several people you admire. What do you admire about them? What have you learned from each person? *Example:* My grandfather laughs a lot and doesn't take life too seriously. I learned from him that it's important to relax.

2. Choose one of the people you discussed in #1. Collect information about his or her life. You can get information by interviewing the person. If he or she is no longer living, interview people who knew him or her. Take notes during the interview.
   Speaking/Listening tip: When you interview someone, avoid asking **"yes/no" questions** ("Did you like that job?"). Instead, ask **open-ended questions** ("What did you think of that job?").

3. Write a five-paragraph reflective essay. Use this organization:
   - Paragraph 1: Write an introduction. Tell who the person is. Give some background about the person. How do you know him or her? What were some important events in his or her life?
   - Paragraph 2: Write one quality you admire. Give examples of this person's actions or attitude that show this quality.
   - Paragraph 3: Write another quality you admire. Give some examples.
   - Paragraph 4: Write a third quality you admire and give examples.
   - Paragraph 5: Write a conclusion. Tell what you learned from this person. How can you apply what this person has taught you to your own life?

4. Share your work with a partner. Use Activity Master 94 (Steps in the Writing Process) on page 121 and Activity Master 97 (Editing Checklist) on page 124 to revise your work and create a final draft.

5. Present your reflective essay to the class. If possible, bring in a photo of the person.

Extend: The next time you write a reflective essay, remember to develop your ideas with examples.

Check your progress:

Listening/Speaking: Did you ask open-ended questions?

Reading: Did you read your partner's essay? Did you provide feedback?

Writing: Did you take notes? Did you give examples and supporting information for each quality you admire?

UNIT 4: ADVICE

Use with student text page 196.

Proverbs

Every culture has proverbs or sayings. The meaning of proverbs is usually not literal but figurative.

In the chart below, write some proverbs you know or find in a resource book in the library. Illustrate your proverbs and write their meaning.

Proverb or saying	Illustration	Meaning
"That's like taking candy from a baby."		That's very easy.
"She speaks with a forked tongue."		She doesn't tell the truth.

UNIT 4: ADVICE

Writing process. Students make an illustrated chart of proverbs as a **pre-writing strategy** to create a poem or short story (page 105).

Listening/Speaking/evaluation. Have partners read their proverbs aloud and discuss and analyze the effect of the language and imagery in the proverb.

Use with student text page 199.

Using Proverbs

1. Combine two or more of the proverbs you wrote on your chart on Activity Master 82. Create a poem or short story from these proverbs. Try to combine them in a surprising way. Write your first draft below.

2. Use Activity Master 94 (Steps in the Writing Process) to revise, edit, and publish your work.

_____

_____

_____

_____

_____

_____

_____

_____

_____

_____

_____

_____

_____

_____

_____

_____

_____

_____

UNIT 4: ADVICE

Writing process.   Ask students to create a poem or short story combining two or more proverbs as they write their first draft.
Listening/Speaking.   Have students read their poems and short stories aloud. Have others respond to them, offering compliments and suggestions for improvement.

Use with student text page 197.

Proverbs and Sayings: Writing a Play

Words to Know

plot   character   script   narrator   proverb   moral   saying

Project Goal: In this unit, you have learned some **proverbs** and **sayings** and discussed what they meant in the poem "Conceit." Now you will write a play that gives a modern-day example of a proverb or saying. Work in small groups.

1. Select one of these proverbs or use one of your own. In your group, read each and discuss what it means. Be sure to include everyone in the discussion.
    - *Slow and steady wins the race.*
    - *Don't judge a man until you have walked a mile in his shoes.*
    - *A penny saved is a penny earned.*
    - *Beauty is only skin deep.*

    In a small group, think of a modern-day situation that illustrates this proverb, **moral,** or saying. Summarize the **plot** in a few sentences. Here is an example for "Slow and steady wins the race."

    Two students are trying to get into college. They need a scholarship. One student studies a little bit every day. Another student only studies the night before. She thinks she can still pass the tests. In the end, the student who studied only the night before doesn't do very well. The student who studied a little bit every day wins the scholarship.
    Moral: Slow and steady wins the race.

2. Now write a play based on your plot. One person will be the **narrator**. The narrator will explain the situation as needed in the scene. He or she will say the proverb or moral as the final line. Use the other characters to show (not tell) the plot. Include a **character** for everyone in the group.

    > **Writing tip:** Write the dialogue in the style of a play. Use a colon after a character's name and then write the dialogue. For example:
    > *Narrator: There were two students at Central High School who needed a college scholarship.*

3. Practice your play in small groups before you perform it for the class. Make sure each person has a copy of the **script**. Speak clearly with an appropriate tone of voice.

Extend: Read fables by Aesop or La Fontaine. Find a fable that has good advice for people today. Share this with the class.

Check your progress:

Listening/Speaking: Did you speak clearly with an appropriate tone of voice?

Reading: Did you read and discuss the meaning of the proverbs with your group?

Writing: Did you summarize the plot before you began writing?

UNIT 4: ADVICE

Use with student text page 200.

Learning from Mistakes

1. Think of some of the mistakes children make because they don't know any better. List these mistakes below.

_____

_____

_____

_____

_____

2. Write a story about a mistake you or someone you know made. What was the mistake? What happened? Did it ever happen again? Use the Editing Checklist (Activity Master 97) to edit your work.

_____

_____

_____

_____

_____

_____

_____

_____

_____

_____

_____

_____

_____

_____

UNIT 4: ADVICE

Writing purposes. Students write a **personal** story about a mistake, and then edit for spelling, grammar, punctuation, and capitalization.

Use with student text page 211.

Narrative and Lyric Poems

Look back over the poems you have read in your student text. Which of the poems do you think are narrative? Which are lyric? Write the titles of the poems on one side of the chart. On the other side of the chart, state if the poem is narrative or lyric. Finally, include a few lines of the poem to support your decision.

Title	Narrative or Lyric

Writing/inquiry/research. Students use writing to **organize and support** what is known about narrative and lyric poetry.

Use with student text page 211.

Story Map of a Lesson from Childhood

1. Choose an event in your childhood that taught you something.
2. Use this Story Map to outline the main elements of the story.

Title: _____	Author: _____
Story Elements	
Characters:	
Setting:	
Initial event:	
Reaction:	
Problem:	
Solution:	
Lesson Learned:	

UNIT 4: ADVICE

Listening/Speaking critically. Encourage students to read their stories aloud and others to listen critically to tell what the lesson is.

Use with student text pages 201–209.

Exaggeration: Writing a Diary Entry

Words to Know

exaggeration	exaggerated	point of view	diary	humor
comparative	simile	metaphor	idiom	

Project Goal: In "La Peseta," the author tells a story from a child's **point of view**. The sights the child describes are **exaggerated** because the world looks different to a child. **Exaggeration** adds **humor** and emotion to the story. You will practice using exaggeration in a **diary** entry.

1. Write five sentences about things that happened yesterday. Use your imagination and exaggerate the incident. Make an exaggeration by using **comparatives, similes, idioms, metaphors,** or *so...that*. Look at the examples on the chart.

What happened	Exaggeration	Structure
I slept through my alarm.	The alarm rang *so* loudly *that* the bed shook, but I didn't wake up.	*so* + adverb + *that*...
I was very hungry.	I was *so* hungry *that* I ate a mountain of spaghetti.	*so* + adjective + *that*...
My book bag was very heavy.	My book bag *was* heavier *than* a pile of rocks.	noun + *to be* + comparative adjective + *than*
I ran to the bus.	I had to *run like a track star* to catch my bus.	simile: use *like* to compare two people or things
I had a substitute teacher in English class.	The substitute *teacher was a giant* with a voice louder than thunder.	metaphor: noun phrase + *is*/*was* + noun phrase

2. Develop your sentences into a diary entry about your day yesterday. Write the paragraph like this:
   Dear Diary,

   What a terrible day yesterday was! The alarm clock rang so loudly that the windows shook, but I didn't wake up. I didn't have time to eat breakfast. I was so hungry by lunchtime that I ate a mountain of spaghetti.

3. Work with a partner to review your diary entry. Use Activity Master 96 on page 123.

4. Make illustrations for your diary entry. The pictures should be as exaggerated as the words. Display the entries in class, read each other's work, and find examples of exaggeration.

Extend: Use exaggeration in other creative writing assignments to add humor or emotion.

Check your progress:

Reading: Did you find examples of comparatives, similes, or metaphors in your partner's work?

Writing: Did you develop your sentences into a paragraph?

Viewing: Did you draw illustrations that are exaggerated?

Use with student text pages 220–221.

Writing People's Speech

Tape two people in your class discussing the game they like the best. Listen to the tape and *transcribe*, or write down, one minute of the discussion. Use the rules below to transcribe the discussion. Use more paper if you run out of room on this page.

How to Transcribe People's Speech in Dialogue and Quotations

1. Start a new paragraph each time a different person speaks.

2. Put quotation marks (" ") before and after the exact words a person speaks.

3. If the person's words are in the middle of a sentence, put a comma before and after the quotation. The comma before is outside the quotation marks (, "). The comma after is inside (,").

4. If another punctuation mark is part of the quotation, include it inside the quotation marks (!"), (.").

Examples:

"I said I'll play," I whined.

"No!" she shouted, and I almost jumped out of my scalp. "It is not so easy anymore."

Writing/conventions.   Students produce legible work with correct use of **quotation** marks.

Copyright © 2001 Heinle & Heinle

UNIT 4: ADVICE

Use with student text page 221.

Story Map: Short Story

1. Plan a story with some memorable characters.
2. Use this Story Map to outline your story's basic elements.

Title: _____ Author:_____	
Story Elements	
Characters:	
Setting:	
Initial event:	
Reaction:	
Problem:	
Solution:	

Writing process. Students use the **pre-writing strategy** of a graphic organizer to plan a story with memorable characters.

UNIT 4: ADVICE

Use with student text pages 213–219.

Pastime or Passion: Describing a Hobby or Game

Words to Know

hobby   pastime   game   equipment   strategy   capture

Project Goal: In "Four Directions," the daughter loved to play chess. It was her **hobby** or "**pastime.**" Popular hobbies include playing games of **strategy** like chess, playing musical instruments, designing a website, or doing artwork. Do you have a hobby? You will demonstrate a hobby, **game,** or pastime for your class.

1. Write the name of your hobby at the top of a chart like this one. In the left column, write "**equipment** or materials" and "rules to follow" or "steps to follow." In the right column, fill in the information.

Chess	
Equipment or materials	chessboard chess pieces
Rules to follow	goal — **capture** the queen

2. Use the information from the chart to write a "how to" paragraph. Begin with a topic sentence. Next, write a sentence telling what materials or things you need. Then write the steps in the order you do them.
    > **Writing tip:** Use words like *first, second, third, next, then,* and *finally* when you write the steps. Use the imperative form of the verb (*Put the chess pieces on the board.*).

3. Search for more information about your hobby. Look for a magazine about your hobby or search the Internet for a website. Bring in some interesting pictures or print out a picture to use with your demonstration.

4. Demonstrate your hobby or game for the class. Bring the things you need to do the activity. Explain the steps or rules.
    > **Listening tip:** Listen carefully when another student is demonstrating a hobby. Ask questions if you don't understand. This will help the student explain the hobby clearly.

Extend: Use a "how to" paragraph when you write reports such as science experiments.

Check your progress:

Listening/Speaking: Did you ask questions when you didn't understand something in your classmates' demonstrations?

Reading: Did you read about your hobby in a magazine or on the Internet?

Writing: Did you use a chart to organize information? Did you use imperative forms of verbs?

Viewing: Did you search magazines or the Internet for pictures and information?

UNIT 4: ADVICE

Use with student text page 227.

The Writing Process: Writing Advice about Hopes and Dreams

1. Pre-writing

Decide on the hopes and dreams you will write about. Then think about your writing, gather ideas and information, and make plans. You might use a cluster map.

2. Drafting

Decide on a form you'll use. Will you write a poem, a story, or an essay? Get your ideas down on paper. Try to write quickly and fluidly. Do not worry now about details like spelling and punctuation. Try a quickwrite.

3. Sharing

Share your writing with a partner or small group. When you respond to others' writing, remember:

First, offer encouragement and tell them the parts you like.

Second, ask questions to help the writer come up with more information or ideas.

Third, offer suggestions for improving or polishing the writing.

4. Revising

After you get ideas and suggestions from your peers and your teacher, add needed information, delete unnecessary information, clarify details, improve word choices, and organize the piece.

5. Editing

Use the Editing Checklist on page 124 to check your own work for improvements needed in spelling, usage, punctuation, arrangement of words on the page, etc. You might like to trade papers with a partner and proof each other's work.

6. Publishing

Share your work with the world! Here are some ways to publish:

* *Put it in a class book about hopes and dreams. Put the book in the class or school library.*
* *Read it aloud to the class.*
* *Post it on the wall in the classroom or hall.*
* *Read it to the school on a video broadcast.*
* *Make an accordion book.*
* *Send it through E-mail.*
* *Submit it to the school paper or literary magazine.*

UNIT 4: ADVICE

Listening/Speaking. Have students read their poems, stories, and essays aloud. Tell them to speak clearly and use appropriate tone of voice. Have others listen to find out what each hope and dream is.

Use with student text pages 223–225.

Advice for the Future: A Graduation Speech

Words to Know

graduate   graduation   speech   inauguration   cluster map

Project Goal: Maya Angelou wrote "On the Pulse of Morning" for a presidential **inauguration**. She encourages people to have hope for the future. She advises people not to fear change. Instead, she tells them to create opportunities. What advice do you have for students who will soon **graduate**? You will write a **graduation speech** giving advice to your classmates.

1. Use a **cluster map** (Activity Master 12, page 15) to brainstorm ideas for your speech. In the circle at the center of your cluster write "Advice to my classmates." Think about advice other people have given you. Think about the hope you have for the future. Think about experiences in high school that helped you. Write all your ideas in the cluster map.

2. Look at your cluster map and pick the three most important or interesting pieces of advice. Add details in the map about why this advice is important to you. Use your own experience. For example, if you volunteered with a club, what was valuable in that experience?

3. Write your speech. Write an introduction, include your three pieces of advice with supporting details, and end with a concluding statement. Edit your speech with a partner. Revise it and write a final draft. Use Activity Masters 96 and 97 on pages 123 and 124.
    Writing tip: Formal language is usually used in a speech. Check your vocabulary and select formal words.

4. Practice your speech with a partner. Ask for help pronouncing words. Practice making eye contact with your partner. When you give your speech to the class, look at your audience.
    Speaking tip: When you give your speech, you should make eye contact. Silently read and remember a sentence, look up at the class, and then say the sentence to your audience. Take more time between sentences. Give your audience time to listen.

Extend: The next time you have to give a speech or an oral report, use this process to prepare, write, and practice.

Check your progress:

Listening/Speaking: Did you make eye contact with your audience?

Reading: Did you identify your three pieces of advice?

Writing: Did you use formal language? Did you revise your speech?

Develop vocabulary and language about diversity with the Making Connections CD-ROM, Unit 8.

UNIT 4: ADVICE

Use with student text page 228.

Venn Diagram

1. Use this Venn diagram to compare and contrast two characters from Unit 4. Write the names on the lines.

2. In each large circle, list ways that the characters are different.

3. Where the circles overlap, list ways they are alike.

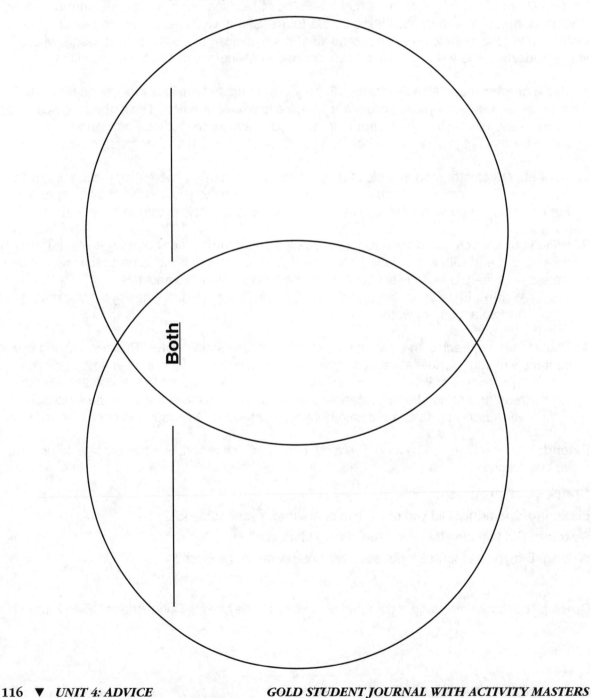

Reading/skim and scan. After students have chosen two characters, have them skim and scan the stories for details to use in their comparisons.

Writing process. Have students use this **graphic organizer** to list the details about the characters.

UNIT 4: ADVICE

Use with student text page 228.

Character Web

1. Use this Character Web to help you focus on one of the characters you will compare. Write the character's name in the circle.

2. List a quality of the character in each box. Then draw a picture that shows that quality.

3. Make another Character Web for the other character.

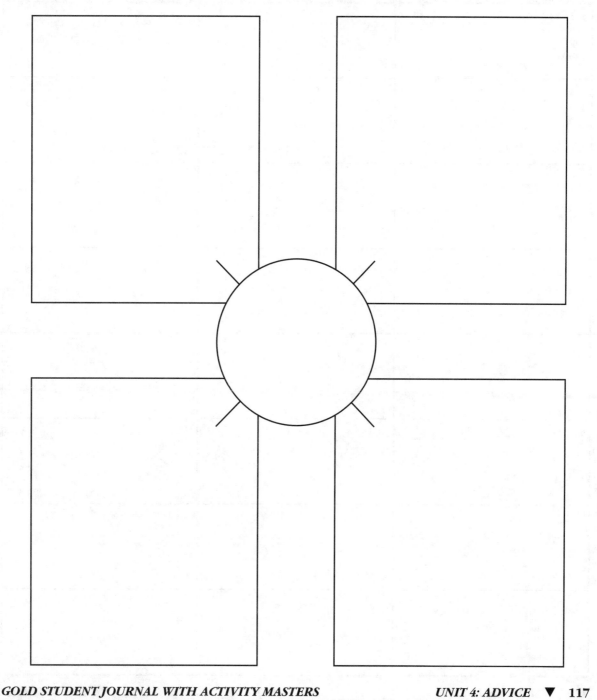

UNIT 4: ADVICE

Reading/skim and scan.   After students have chosen two characters, have them skim and scan the stories for details to use in their comparisons.

Writing process.   Have students use this **graphic organizer** to list the details about the characters.

Use with student text page 227.

Advice in Unit 4

Look back over all the selections in Unit 4. In each selection, the author or one of the characters offered advice. Fill in the chart below with the advice offered in this unit.

Title	Person Offering Advice	Advice

Writing/inquiry/research. Students use writing as a study tool to clarify and remember information about how authors or characters offer advice in Unit 4.

UNIT 4: ADVICE

Copyright © 2001 Heinle & Heinle

(93) ACTIVITY MASTER

Write an Autobiographical Narrative

Words to Use

lesson   learned   This experience taught me…   As a result…

Goal: You will write a story about a lesson you learned in your life. Follow each step carefully.

1. Read the prompt, or topic. What will you be writing about? Who is your audience? Focus on the purpose of your writing: to tell a true story about a lesson you learned.

Prompt: Write a true story about something that happened to you. Choose an experience that taught you a lesson in life. Tell what happened and the lesson you learned. You will share your story with the class.

2. Read these examples. Then list two or three events from your life. Choose one to write about.

EVENT	RESULT	LESSON
Left my bus money at home	Had to walk three miles in the rain	Always carry extra bus money with me
Didn't sign up for classes on time	Couldn't get into the art class I really wanted to take	Sign up early

3. Next, organize your story. Use an outline. Decide on a way to begin your story that will get your reader's attention. Then list the event, the result, and the lesson you learned from it. Finally, decide how you will end your story.

4. Write a draft of five paragraphs. (Don't forget to indent!) Write five sentences for paragraphs 2, 3, and 4. Use words from the Words to Use list above.

   • Paragraph 1: Start your story with a topic sentence. Get your reader's attention. Tell who, what, where, and when briefly.

   • Paragraph 2: Tell what happened to you. Start with: *When I was….*

   • Paragraph 3: Tell what the result was. Start with: *As a result….*

   • Paragraph 4: Tell the lesson you learned. Start with: *This experience taught me….*

   • Paragraph 5: Write a conclusion. You might summarize how you learned the lesson.

Work with a partner and give each other feedback. Be sure to tell one thing you liked and one way your partner could improve the story. Use Activity Master 96 on page 123.

5. Write your final draft. Compare lessons learned with those of your classmates.

UNIT 4: ADVICE

Writing/autobiographical narrative. Students write a five-paragraph narrative.
Writing process/pre-writing/drafting. Have students list ideas, choose one, and then make an outline as **pre-writing** and **drafting** steps in the writing process.

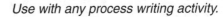

Use with any process writing activity.

ACTIVITY
94
MASTER

Steps in the Writing Process

1. Pre-writing
Think about your writing, gather ideas and information, and make plans. You might use:
A Story Map
A Character Web
A Cluster Map
A Venn Diagram

2. Drafting
Get your ideas down on paper. Try to write quickly and fluidly, and not to worry now about details like spelling and punctuation. Try a quickwrite.

3. Sharing
Share your writing with a partner or small group. When you respond to others' writing, remember:
First, offer encouragement and tell them the parts you like.
Second, ask questions to help the writer come up with more information or ideas.
Third, offer suggestions for improving or polishing the writing.

4. Revising
After you get ideas and suggestions from your peers and your teacher, add needed information, delete unnecessary information, clarify details, improve word choices, and organize the piece.

5. Editing
Use the Editing Checklist on page 124 to check your own work for improvements needed in spelling, usage, punctuation, arrangement of words on the page, etc. You might like to trade papers with a partner and proof one another's work.

6. Publishing
Share your work with the world! Here are some ways to publish:
- *Put it in a book in the class or school library.*
- *Read it aloud to the class.*
- *Post it on the wall in the classroom or hall.*
- *Read it to the school on a video broadcast.*
- *Make an accordion book.*
- *Send it through E-mail.*
- *Submit it to the school paper or literary magazine.*

Writing process.   Have students follow the writing steps outlined on the chart to self-check and then check their peers' writing.

Use after group activities.

Group Activity Evaluation

Complete this form after you work in a group.

MY CONTRIBUTIONS		
Added ideas to the project	☐ Yes ☐ No	**Examples:**
Worked well with other group members	☐ Yes ☐ No	**Examples:**
Contributed fair share of work	☐ Yes ☐ No	**Examples:**
Took leadership roles	☐ Yes ☐ No	**Examples:**
Encouraged other group members	☐ Yes ☐ No	**Examples:**
Other:	☐ Yes ☐ No	**Examples:**

How well did your whole group work together?

_____

_____

_____

_____

_____

_____

_____

Listening/Speaking and Writing/evaluation. Encourage students to use the form above to evaluate their participation in a group. Have them set goals for other group writing activities.

Use with any process writing activity.

ACTIVITY 96 MASTER

Responding to Peers' Writing: EQS

E: Encourage	Q: Ask Questions	S: Suggestions

Help your partner know what he or she is doing right. Be specific.
 	
"I liked the surprise at the end the best."
 	
"You used some very interesting words in this sentence."
 	
"This poem made me think about my homeland."
	Ask questions when you would like more information. Ask questions when something isn't quite clear.
	
	"Why did your grandmother give you that picture?"
	
	"What do you mean, 'He went back'? Where did he go?"
		Ask your partner if he or she would like some suggestions.
		    If your partner says "Yes," offer suggestions to make the writing better.
		    Always let your partner choose whether or not to use your ideas.
		    Let your partner own his or her writing.
		
		"You might try saying 'My dog is fat' another way. How about 'My dog looks like a sausage with four legs'?"
		
		"What if you changed these two sentences around?"

Read your partner's selection. Use EQS to fill in the boxes.

Name: _____   **Partner's Name:** _____

E: Encourage	Q: Ask Questions	S: Suggestions

RESOURCE PAGES

Writing/evaluation. Students evaluate peers' writing.

Use with all writing projects.

Editing Checklist

Edit for:	☑ Yes	Comments
Mechanics *Form* • Does the piece use correct form and arrangement on the page? *Capitalization* • Are capital letters used appropriately?	☐ ☐	
Spelling and Word Choice • Did you check the spelling of all the words you weren't sure about? • Are your words exact, interesting, varied, and needed? • Did you use strong verbs and adjectives?	☐ ☐ ☐	
Grammar *Sentences* • Are sentences complete (no comma splices or sentence fragments)? • Do sentences make sense? • Do nouns, verbs, and adjectives agree?	☐ ☐ ☐	
Organization and Content • Is your plot or other organization clear? • Do you have a strong, interesting beginning? • Is your plot/content logical? • Do you vary your sentences and words for interest? • Do you have a strong, interesting ending? • Is your purpose for writing clear?	☐ ☐ ☐ ☐ ☐ ☐	
Style • Does your style fit the audience? • Does your style suit the occasion? • Does your style match the voice in your writing?	☐ ☐ ☐	

Writing/process and evaluation. Have students edit their writing and that of others using the **Editing Checklist** above.

Use after presentations and performances.

Performance and Presentation Evaluation Chart

Informative presentations give information.

Persuasive presentations express an opinion based on reasons and facts.

Artistic performances are plays, songs, and dances.

Media presentations are viewed through video, movie, TV, Internet, and art presentations.

Directions: Listen to presentations and watch performances by peers, public figures, and media presenters. Take notes in the chart below:

Topic	Type Informative? Persuasive? Artistic? Media?	Details What I liked or disliked
Newscast about The Wife's Story	Television newscast performed and videotaped	I liked how the reporter got the attention of the audience and the interview with the wife.

Listening/speaking/evaluation. Students evaluate informative and persuasive presentations of peers, public figures, and media presenters. Students also evaluate artistic performances of peers, public presenters, and media presentations.

RESOURCE PAGES

Use with any text that involves inductive reasoning.

School Classrooms:
Inductive Reasoning

In **inductive reasoning**, you think about things or details and how they fit together. You do this when you read to help you understand what you are reading. Look at the pictures below and think about where each is used.

For example, you use *test tubes* in a science class.

test tubes   violin   paintbrush   soccer ball   ruler   sheet music   microscope

pencils   protractor   frog   paints   keyboard   calculator   sneakers

Write each thing pictured under the correct school subject.

SCIENCE	PHYSICAL EDUCATION	ART	MUSIC	MATH
Test tubes				

Now, use inductive reasoning to write about the things you use in your classes.

In science class, I use _____

_____

_____

_____

Reading/analysis/evaluation. Students analyze text to determine the mode of reasoning used, such as **induction** and deduction.

Use with any text that involves deductive reasoning.

School Classrooms: Deductive Reasoning

In **deductive reasoning**, you think about the whole picture. You do this to discover details about what you are reading. Read the map below. Answer the questions that follow.

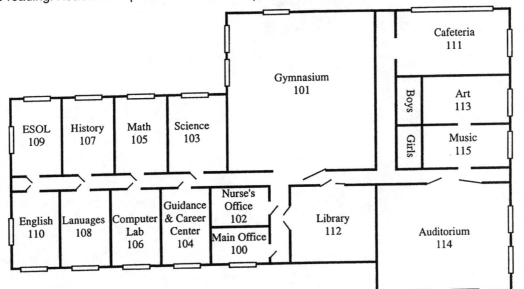

Read and write.

1. (example) Where is biology class?

It's in room 103.

2. Where is band practice?

It's . . .

3. Where is physical education?

4. Where is lunch?

5. Where is geometry class?

6. Where can you do research on the Internet?

With a partner, draw a map of your own school. Describe your map in class.

RESOURCE PAGES

Reading/analysis/evaluation.   Students analyze text to determine the mode of reasoning used, such as induction and **deduction**.
Second language acquisition/speaking. Students describe school room locations.